Chronology

Of Texas History

ENTRANCE TO THE ALAMO CHAPEL

— Courtesy Daughters of the Republic of Texas

Chronology

Of
Texas
History

By
Donald W. Whisenhunt

EAKIN PRESS ★ BURNET, TEXAS

To

Betsy, Donald, and Ben

With Love

SAM HOUSTON, first president of Texas and later governor, from a portrait by William Henry Huddle in the rotunda of the Texas State Capitol.

— Courtesy Texas State Library

INTRODUCTION

Since 1952 *The Handbook of Texas* has been the definitive encyclopedic work on Texas history. It is unequaled in the United States since no other state has a publication that can compare with it. Its value has increased even more since volume three was published in 1976. The Texas State Historical Association is to be commended for this valuable service to the citizens of Texas. The Association, apparently, plans to issue a new volume every ten years or so to fill in gaps, correct errors in earlier volumes, and to keep a running historical record.

As a professional historian who has lived in several states and who has taken an interest in the local history of those areas, I found a dearth of readily available information in comparison to Texas. Although *The Handbook of Texas* is meant to be a ready reference — truly an encyclopedia — it has also been the starting point for many professional historians who later developed significant research projects.

For many laymen and professional historians, the placing of an event in an exact chronological position is important but sometimes difficult to do. Unfortunately, there is no readily available source for such information.

The purpose of this book is to provide a chronology of Texas history. It is keyed directly to *The Handbook*. All three volumes were read carefully to extract all significant dates. No other sources were consulted. Obviously there are many dates of events that are not included here. Very early the decision was made not to consult any source other than *The Handbook* because the task would become a never-ending one.

As any recent historian is painfully aware, the research on Texas in the twentieth century is not as extensive as it should be. Consequently, the detail available in *The Handbook* is not as comprehensive on recent events. A decision was made, therefore, to end this chronology with 1920. If this first volume is successful and fills a need, a second volume covering the period since 1920, a project requiring much more research, will be published.

Certain other limitations should be noted. A decision was made not to include dates from the biographical sketches in *The Handbook* unless the subject was a very significant individual in Texas history,

EMILY DICKINSON, survivor of the Alamo.

— *Courtesy the University of Texas Library*

such as Sam Houston or William Barret Travis. The focus, therefore, is upon events instead of people. Another limitation is the fact that many of the articles in *The Handbook* do not specify exact dates of events. Even though further research could have supplied the exact month and day in many instances, the decision was to stay only with *The Handbook*. These events, therefore, are grouped together at the beginning of the appropriate year.

It should also be noted that this book is not intended to give you exhaustive description of the events included. Were that to be done, it would be merely a repetition of *The Handbook*. Instead, it is designed to whet the reader's appetite for more information. If the reader would like to know more about a specific event he can go to *The Handbook* itself or to a more specialized history of the event or period.

Without question, errors will creep into a book of this type despite scrupulous efforts to avoid them. Hopefully, readers will inform us of the errors; should there be a need for a second edition, the errors can be corrected. Furthermore, if interest warrants a second edition, the entries could be expanded beyond the dates in *The Handbook*.

Texans of all types, we hope, will find this book of interest. It is not designed as a scholarly volume although every effort was made to be accurate. Neither is the book designed to be read in narrative fashion. It is a reference work to be used as a ready guide to Texas history. Hopefully, persons interested in Texas history will also find it to be a book for browsing since that can produce some surprising facts. It is our sincere hope that this book will be accepted for what it is, not for what it is not. Hopefully, it can be of interest to the professional and amateur historian as well as to the general public.

Although this is the work of the compiler who accepts all responsibility for accuracy, at least two persons need to be acknowledged. Dr. Tuffly Ellis, Director of the Texas State Historical Association, provided encouragement through every phase of the project. Mr. Ed Eakin is the person most responsible for the project coming to fruition. While other publishers were afraid of the project because it was somewhat unorthodox, Mr. Eakin was enthusiastic from the beginning, so much so that he was willing to undertake the financial risk involved in such an unusual book. His faith was very encouraging.

Above all, my family deserves credit for living with this project for over a year. My wife, Betsy, has always been supportive, and my sons, Donald and Ben, have always been proud, if uncertain, of their father's work.

Tyler, Texas
February 1, 1981

Donald W. Whisenhunt

STEPHEN F. AUSTIN'S MAP OF 1835

Chronology

Of Texas History

900

Pueblo-building people moved into the Canadian River Valley in the Texas Panhandle

1528

The following Indian tribes reported along the Texas coast (including Matagorda and Galveston Islands) by Alvar Nuñez, Cabeza de Vaca: Atayo, Coaque, Doguene, Han, Maliacone, Quevene, Quitole
November 5. Alonso de Castillo Maldonado's ship wrecked on the Texas coast one day before Alvar Nuñez, Cabeza de Vaca's ship suffered the same fate

1540

Teya Indians reported in Texas by the Coronado Expedition
January 6. Francisco Vázquez de Coronado appointed by Viceroy Mendoza to lead an expedition to the seven cities of Cibola.
April 22. Coronado Expedition set out from Mexico

1541

Palo Duro Canyon supposedly first seen by Coronado

1542

The expedition of Luis de Moscoso reported contact with the following Indian tribes in Texas: Caddo, Hacanac, Kadodacho, Lacane
May 21. Hernando De Soto died on the Mississippi River and was succeeded by Luis de Moscoso de Alvarado and it became known as the Moscoso Expedition

1543

Oil first discovered in Texas by Europeans when Luis de Moscoso used oil seepage near Nacogdoches

1

1581

June 6. The Rodriguez-Chamuscado Expedition started out from Mexico

1583

Antonio de Espejo reported Jumano Indians on the Pecos River
Antonio de Espejo named the area at the Conchos and Rio Grande rivers inhabited by the Jumano Indians La Junta de los Rios

1584

Tanpachoa Indians reported on the Rio Grande near present El Paso

1590

Tepelguan Indians reported in Texas by Gaspar Castaño de Sosa

1650

Captain Diego del Castillo led an expedition from Santa Fe to explore north central Texas
Escanjaque Indians reported on either the Concho or upper Colorado River by Hernán Martín and Diego del Castillo

1654

Diego de Guadalajara placed in command of an expedition to explore the Concho River area

1659

The Manso Indians were settled at El Paso at the mission of Nuestra Señora de Guadalupe de los Mansos

1665

Cacaxtle Indians attacked by the Spanish who crossed the Rio Grande into Texas
Bobole Indians reported in South Texas

1670

Muruam Indians reported in Texas by Damian Massanet

1674

Manos Colorados and Ocana Indians reported north of the Rio Grande in Texas

1675

Quarai Indians fled from hostile Apaches from New Mexico to the El Paso area

Cocoma Indians reported as occasionally crossing the Rio Grande into Texas

The following Indian tribes reported in Texas: Pachaque, Pataguo (along the Rio Grande), Pinanaca

The following Indian tribes reported in Texas by the Bosque-Larios Expedition led by Fernando del Bosque: Bibit (in present Kinney County), Ervipiame, Espopolame, Gueiquesale, Hape, Heniocane, Hume (near present Eagle Pass), Pinanca, Taimamar (sometimes called Taimamare), Yorica

April 30. Bosque-Larios Expedition set out for Texas from Mexico to Christianize the Indians

May 11. Bosque-Larios Expedition reached the Rio Grande

May 25. Bosque-Larios Expedition reached present Edwards County where a decision was made to return to Mexico

1680

Pinto and Piro Indians moved by the Spanish to Socorro del Sur near present El Paso

Silver first discovered in Texas in the El Paso area

The Tiguex Indians moved from New Mexico to El Paso

1682

First Spanish mission in Texas, Corpus Christi de la Isleta, established

Nuestra Señora de la Concepción del Socorro (also known as Purisiima Concepción del Socorro and as Socorro del Sur) established near El Paso

Tigua Indians settled near present El Paso

April 8. La Salle claimed the Mississippi River and its tributaries for the French king, Louis XIV

1683

The following Indian tribes reported in Texas by Juan Sabeata: Peñunde (on the Nueces River), Quide, Quioborique, Quitaca, Tohaha, Unojita, Utaca

The following Indian tribes reported in Texas: Agua Sucia ("dirty water"), Arihuman (West Texas), Bean, Borobama, Caimane (in the Pecos River area), Come, Comocara, Flechas Feas, Geobari, Janaque, Los Surdos, Mana, Mano, Miembros Largos, Muele, Neuz, Obori (sometimes called Obozi), Pescado, Tishim, Tixemu (at El Paso), Toapa, Toapari

December. La Navidad en las Cruces established as a temporary mission for the Jumano Indians in present Presidio County

1684

Pamorano Indians reported north of Laredo by Manuel Orozco y Berra

The following Indian tribes reported in Texas by Juan Domínguez de Mendoza: Aba, Abau (on the Edwards Plateau), Achubale, Aguioa, Aieli, Anchimo, Arcos Tuertos, Asen Arcos, Bajunero, Beitonijure, Bobida, Caula, Colabrote, Conchamucha, Cujaco, Cujalo, Cunquebaco (near present San Angelo), Detobiti, Diju, Echancote, Flechas Chiquitas, Hanasine (near present San Angelo), Hinehi, Hinsa, Huane, Huicasique, Inhame, Isucho, Jedionda, Novrach, Ororoso, Pagaiam, Paiabuna, Patzau, Pojue, Pucha, Pucham, Puguahiane, Pulcha, Quicuchabe, Quisaba, Quitaca, Siacucha, Suajo, Suma, Teanda, Tojuma, Torgme, Unojita, Ylame, Yoyehi

March 16. San Clemente Mission established by Juan Domingo de Mendoza near present Ballinger

June 12. San Francisco de los Julimes Mission established near present Presidio by Juan Domínguez de Mendoza

1685

January 1. La Salle landed in the vicinity of present Jefferson County

January 20. La Salle made his first headquarters in Texas

February. Fort St. Louis established in the Matagorda Bay area by Réne Robert Cavelier, Sieur de la Salle

1686

Nabedache Indians reported in present Houston County by Henri Joutel

1687

The following Indian tribes reported in Texas: Ahehouen (north of Matagorda Bay), Anachorema, Annaho (on the Red River), Palaquesson (near the Brazos River), Quara (on the Lavaca River), Taraha (on the Red River)

The following Indian tribes reported in Texas by Henri Joutel: Daquio, Datcho, Erigoanna (near Matagorda Bay), Haqui, Hianagouy, Hiantatsi, Kabaye (Matagorda Bay-Colorado River area), Keremen (on the Colorado River), Kironona, Mayeye (on the San Gabriel and Little Rivers), Meracouman (near the Colorado River), Nadamin (near the Red River), Ointemarhen, Omenaosse, Petao, Spichehat

The following Indian tribes reported in Texas by the La Salle Expedition: Caiaban, Cannaha, Cannahio, Cantey, Cassia (on the Red River), Erigoanna, Kannehouan (near the Colorado River),

4

Kanohatino, Neche (in present Cherokee County), Pamoque, Panequo, Quinet, Quiouaha, Tahiannihouq, Tchanhié

Nabiri Indians reported in Texas by Fray Anastasius Douay

1689

The following Indian tribes reported in Texas: Emet (near the lower Guadalupe River), Mescale (near the Nueces River), Quem (near Matagorda Bay)

Telamene Indians reported in Texas by Henri Joutel

The following Indian tribes reported in Texas by Damian Massanet: Samampac and Sampanal (both near the Nueces River)

1690

Llanos-Cárdenas Expedition dispatched to investigate the settlement made by La Salle

Nuestro Padre San Francisco de los Tejas Mission established under the name, San Francisco de los Tejas Mission, in present Hamilton County

Spanish drove two hundred head of cattle to San Francisco de los Tejas, possibly the first cattle brought to Texas

The following Indian tribes reported in Texas: Cabia, Ebahamo, Manam (on the Guadalupe River), Manico (on the Frio River in present Medina County), Naaman, Nacau (at San Francisco de los Tejas Mission), Paac (on the Nueces River), Paachiqui (on the Nueces River), Pachal (on the Nueces River), Pacuache (on the southern edge of the Edwards Plateau), Paguan, Panasiu (on the Guadalupe River), Papanac (on the Nueces River), Pastaloca (on the Nueces River), Payaya (near San Antonio), Payuguan (on the Nueces River), Pitahay (on the Frio River), Pulacuam (on either the Medina or San Antonio River), Semonan

The following Indian tribes reported in Texas by Alonso de León: Caisquetebano, Toaa, Too

The following Indian tribes reported in Texas by Damian Massanet: Emet (near San Antonio), Manico, Paachiqui, Pasteal, Pataguo (near the Nueces River), Patzau, Putaay, Sana, Tecahuiste, Tojo

Paouite Indians reported in Texas by Pierre and Jean Talion

Quinet Indians were not heard of again after this date

September 12. Santísimo Nombre de María Mission founded on the Neches River by Fray Francisco Casañas de Jesús María

1691

The following Indian tribes reported in Texas: Anao, Bata, Caai, Cagaya, Canabatinu, Canonioiba, Canonizochitoui, Canu, Caquixadaquix, Casiba, Cataqueza, Caxo, Caynaaya (east of San Antonio),

Datana, Dico, Guasa, Odoesmade, Pacpul (in present Maverick County), Quibaga, Quiguaya, Quiutcanuaha, Sana (northeast of San Antonio), Sico, Teniba, Tobo, Vidix, Vinta, Xanna, Zauanito, Zonomi

The following Indian tribes reported in Texas by Damian Massanet in the vicinity of the Nueces River: Ocana, Paac, Pastaloca, Pitahay, Vanca

Mepayaya and Nabeyxa Indians reported in Texas by Francisco de Jesús María

The Old San Antonio Road (known also as the King's Highway and the Camino Real) blazed by Domingo Terán de los Rios

1693

The following Indian tribes reported in Texas: Arcos Buenos, Arcos Pordidos, Arcos Tirados, Borrado, Cabellos Blancos, Cabeza, Canaq, Casas Moradas, Colas Largas, Come Cibolas, Conejo, Cruiamo, Dientes Alazanes, Guacali, Macocoma (near present Presidio), Mamuya, Manos Sordos, Mapoch, Mesquite, Pajarito, Piedras Blancas, Pinole, Polacme (near present Presidio), Satatu, Siniple, Sinoreja, Suahuache, Suana, Tepachuache

Obozi Indians reported on the Nueces River by Juan Sabeata

Piedras Blancas Indians reported in Texas by Gregorio Salinas

1696

Hiabu Indians reported by Alonso de León in the Laredo area

1698

Cenizo Indians reported near Eagle Pass

1699

The following Indian tribes reported in Texas: Ismiquilpa, Mahuame (near present Eagle Pass), Xarame

1700

Chaquantie Indians reported living on the Red River

March 1. San Francisco Solano Mission founded near the San Juan Bautista Mission

1701

Pachaloco Indians reported in Texas

1703

Pakawa Indians reported in Texas

1706

Tet Indians reported living near present Eagle Pass

1707

The following Indian tribes reported in Texas: Ervipiame (west of Brazos River), Mariame and Muruam (both near present Eagle Pass)

Diego Ramón sent on a punitive expedition against the Ranchería Grande Indians

1708

The following Indian tribes reported in Texas: Pasqual, Pitalac (on the Rio Grande), Pomulum (on the Rio Grande), Teaname (near present Eagle Pass), Xeripam, Ybdacax, Yemé, Ymic, Ysbupue (near Eagle Pass on the Rio Grande)

The following Indian tribes reported in Texas by Isidoro Felix de Espinosa: Tamcan (on the lower Rio Grande), Tet

1709

The following Indian tribes reported in Texas: Sijame (near San Antonio), Siupam (near San Antonio), Tusolivi (on the Colorado River southeast of present Austin), Yojuane

1715

The mission pueblo El Señor San José founded near present Presidio

1716

The following established by Domingo Ramón: Nuestra Señora de la Purísima Concepción de los Hainai Mission (in present Nacogdoches County), Nuestra Señora de los Dolores de los Ais Mission (also known as Nuestra Señora de los Dolores and as Dolores Mission), Nuestra Señora de los Dolores de los Tejas Presidio (also known as Presidio de los Dolores and as Presidio de los Tejas), San José de los Nazonis Mission, San Miguel de Linares de los Adaes Mission

The following Indian tribes reported in Texas: Mescal, Nacachau, Nacau (near Nacogdoches), Nacogdoche (at Nuestra Señora de Guadalupe de los Nacogdoches Mission), Nacono (at San Francisco de los Neches Mission), Neche, Pamaya, Saracuam

Name of San Francisco de los Tejas Mission changed to Nuestro Padre San Francisco de los Tejas Mission when it was reestablished by Domingo Ramón

Nuestra Señora del Pilar de Nacogdoches was the name given to the town of Nacogdoches when it was established by the Spanish

Nasoni Indians had the mission of San José de los Nazones established for them

The mission of San Francisco de los Neches established for the Nacachau Indians

Domingo Ramón reported Ervipiame Indians west of the Trinity River

Texas was known as the New Philippines

July 9. Nuestra Señora de Guadalupe de los Nacogdoches Mission founded by Domingo Ramón for the Nacogdoche Indians

December. Martín de Alarcón appointed governor of the province of Texas

1718

The following Indian tribes reported in Texas: Huyuguan (near present Austin County), Manos Prietas (at San Antonio de Valero Mission), Payaya (at San Antonio de Valero Mission), Piniquu, Terocodame (at San Francisco Solano Mission), Xarame (at San Antonio de Valero Mission)

May 1. Mission of San Antonio de Valero (the Alamo) established in San Antonio by Fray Antonio de San Buenaventura Olivares

May 5. San Antonio de Bexar Presidio founded by Martín de Alarcón near the Alamo

May 5. Martín de Alarcón founded the Villa de Bexar (present San Antonio)

October 14. San Francisco de Valero, an Indian pueblo, organized by Martín de Alarcón

1719

The following Indian tribes reported in Texas: Caux (in vicinity of Galveston Bay), Nasoni (under French influence), Sama (at San Antonio de Valero Mission), Sumi (at San Antonio de Valero Mission), Tonkawa (near present Texarkana), Wichita

The following tribes reported in Texas by Bernard de la Harpe: Kichai (on the Canadian River), Nacaniche, Yscani

A group of the Natchitoch Indians moved from Louisiana into northeast Texas

April. St. Louis de Caddodacho established on the Red River in Bowie County by Bernard de la Harpe

1720

The following Indian tribes reported in Texas: Aguastaya, Camama, Cana (at San José y San Miguel De Aguayo Mission), Mesquite (at San Antonio de Valero Mission or the Alamo), Pastia (at San José y San Miguel de Aguayo Mission), Payuguan (at San Antonio de Valero Mission), Sulujame

First battle of Bandera Pass fought with Apache Indians

February 23. San José y San Miguel de Aguayo Mission established by Captain Juan Valdez and Father Antonio Margil. de Jesús

1721

Los Adaes, near present Robeline, Louisiana, became colonial capital of Spanish Texas

Deadose Indians reported living on the Trinity River

March 20. The Aguayo Mission to reoccupy Texas crossed the Rio Grande

April 4. Nuestra Señora de Loreto Presidio established near La Bahía Mission by the Aguayo Expedition

1722

The following Indian tribes reported in Texas: Aranama (at Espíritu Santo de Zuñiga Mission), Coapite and Cujane (near Matagorda Bay)

Nuestra Señora de Espíritu Santo de Zuñiga Mission (also known as La Bahía Mission) founded by the Aguayo Expedition

March 12. San Francisco Xavier de Naxara Mission established by the Marquis de Aguayo near San Antonio

June 13. Marquis de Aguayo recommended to the king of Spain that families from the Canary Islands be used to populate the province of Texas

1723

Taracone Indians reported living in East Texas by Andrés G. Barcia Carballedo y Zuñiga

1726

Muruam and Nonapho Indians reported at San Antonio de Valero (the Alamo) Mission

1727

The following Indian tribes reported in Texas: Pampopa (on the Nueces River), Pasalve, Patacal (crossed from Mexico to Texas), Pita (in the San Antonio area)

1728

The following Indian tribes reported in Texas: Quanataguo (at San Antonio de Valero Mission), Tucara, Tumpzi

1730

Tacame Indians reported in Texas by Juan Agustín Morfi

The following Indian tribes reported in Texas: Nigco (at San An-

A BUILDING from Fort Leaton near Presidio as it appeared about 1936.
— *Photo by Bartlett Cocke, Sr., San Antonio.*
Copy from The University of Texas Institute of Texan Cultures.

tonio de Valero Mission), Pajalat (near the San Antonio River), Sepuncó (at San Antonio de Valero Mission), Taztasagonie (north of San Antonio)

1731

The following Indian tribes reported in Texas: Orejone (near San Antonio), Pajalat and Siquipil (at San Antonio), Tilijae (at San Juan Capistrano Mission), Tilpacopal (near San Antonio), Tiopane, Venado (at San Juan Capistrano Mission)

San José de los Nazonis Mission moved to San Antonio and renamed San Juan Capistrano Mission

Nuestra Señora de la Purísima Concepción de Acuña Mission moved from East Texas to San Antonio

March 5. San Francisco de la Espada Mission located on the San Antonio River

March 9. First group of Canary Islanders led by Juan Leal Goras arrived to settle San Antonio

1732

Chenti Indians associated with the Lipan and other Apache groups

Pressure from the Apaches had driven the Ervipiame Indians to the area between the Brazos and Navasota rivers

Yxandi Indians reported living in Texas

1733

The following Indian tribes reported in Texas: Patalca (at San Antonio), Pachalaque and Patumaca (at Nuestra Señora de la Purísima Concepción de Acuña)

1736

Parchina and Pelone Indians reported on the lower Rio Grande by Pedro de Rivera

1737

The following Indian tribes reported in Texas: Arahoma (at San Francisco de la Espada Mission), Sencase (at San Antonio de Valero Mission), Tacame (at three different missions), Tinapihuaya

1738

Pausane Indians reported at San Antonio

1740

The following Indian tribes reported at San Antonio de Valero

Mission (the Alamo): Cava, Menenquen, Tenu, Tetzino, Toho, Ujuiap, Zorquan

The **Mallet** Expedition, led by Pierre and Paul Mallet, passed through the Texas Panhandle on its way back from New Mexico to New Orleans

1741

Ujuiap Indians reported in Texas

1743

Paguanan and Pasnacanes Indians reported at the mission of San Antonio de Valero

1744

May 8. The cornerstone of the chapel at the Alamo was laid

1746

San Francisco Xavier de Horcasitas Mission established
Pajaseque Indians reported near Corpus Christi

1748

The following Indian tribes reported in Texas: Anathagua, Anchose, Apapax, Atia, Atiasnogue, Cancepne, Caso, Geote, Mayeye (on the San Gabriel River near Rockdale), Pastate, Yojuane

June 3. Pedro del Barrio Junco y Espriella named governor *ad interim* of Texas

1749

The following Indian tribes reported in Texas: Akokisa (at San Ildefonso Mission near present Rockdale), Bidai (at San Francisco Xavier de Horcasitas Mission), Patiri (near present Rockdale), Tamique (near present Goliad)

Spanish Governors' Palace constructed in San Antonio
February 25. San Ildefonso Mission established in present Milam County

April. Nuestra Señora de la Candelaria Mission established near present San Gabriel

1750

Some of the Emet Indians were at San Antonio de Valero Mission
Esquien and Estepisa Indians entered the Mission of Nuestra Señora de la Candelaria

Tup Indians reported on the San Gabriel River
Tiopine Indians became known as the Chayopine Indians
Spanish produced salt in present Hudspeth and Culberson counties

August 22. Nuestra Señora de Dolores founded in present Zapata County

1751

Copane Indians reported on the Texas coast
Deadose Indians represented at the San Ildefonso Mission
March 30. San Francisco Xavier Presidio formally approved by the viceroy

1754

Pasnacan Indians reported in South Texas
Tucubante Indians reported near Eagle Pass
Aguajuani Indians reported in the Nacogdoches area
November. Nuestra Señora del Rosario Mission (also known as Santísimo Rosario, Nuestra Señora del Rosario de los Cujanes Mission, and Rosario Mission) founded near present Goliad

1755

The following Indian tribes reported in Texas: Sampanal and Sanipao (at San Antonio), Tov, Tup (at San Antonio de Valero Mission)

1756

Manos de Perro Indians reported at San Antonio
Nuestra Señora de Guadalupe Mission established near present New Braunfels
Nuestra Señora de la Luz Mission (also known as Nuestra Señora de la Luz del Orcoquisac or as the Orcoquisac Mission) established near present Anahuac
August 21. Angel de Martos y Navarrete appointed governor of Texas

1757

The following Indian tribes reported in Texas: Pinto (in present Hidalgo County), Tepemaca (in Webb County), Tlaxcalan (at San Sabá Mission)
April. San Sabá de la Santa Cruz Mission established near present Menard

1759

Taovaya Indians reported living on the Red River

1760

The following Indian tribes reported in Texas: Manos de Perro (on the lower Rio Grande), Siaguan (at San Antonio de Valero Mission)

The **following** Indian tribes reported in Texas by Fray Bartholomé García: Pausane (near San Antonio), Sanipao, Venado

1761

October 4. Moses Austin born at Durham, Connecticut

1762

Nuestra Señora de la Candelaria del Cañon Mission established near present Barksdale
Yprande Indians reported at San Antonio de Valero Mission
January 23. San Lorenzo de la Santa Cruz Mission (also known as El Cañon Mission) founded in present Edwards County

1764

Orancho and Uracha Indians reported at San Antonio de Valero Mission

1767

The Huane Indians reported in Texas by Gaspar José de Solís
The probable first Irishman in Texas, Hugo O'Conor, became governor *ad interim* of Texas

1768

February. Fray Gaspar José de Solís visited the Carrizo Indian tribe on the Nueces River near present Corpus Christi

1770

Peticado Indians reported living in Texas

1771

Cantona Indians associated with Wichita Indians east of present Waco
The absorption of the Jumano Indians with the Lipan Indians had been completed

1772

Main village of Kichai Indians located near present Palestine
Kitachai Indians reported living near present Palestine
San Antonio made capital of Texas

1776

August 22. The northern frontier provinces of Mexico or New Spain were separated under new authority and called the Provincias Internas

1777

Skidi Pawnee Indians reported living on the Red River

14

1779

Athanase de Méziéres named governor of Texas

Jotar Indians reported living near Nacogdoches by Athanase de Méziéres

The Old Stone Fort built in Nacogdoches by Gil Antonio Ibarvo

1780

Pamoque Indians reported living on the coast at the mouth of the Nueces River

Tampacuaze Indians reported living on the lower Texas coast

1781

Tejas Indians reported living in Texas

Tlascopsel Indians reported in Texas by Juan Agustín Morfi, but he changed the spelling from Lacopsele

1784

Mulato Indians reported at the San José y San Miguel de Aguayo Mission

1785

Cabra Indians reported near Nuestra Señora del Espíritu Santo de Zuñiga Mission

Cachopostale Indians entered the San José y San Miguel de Aguayo Mission

Gincape Indians reported in Texas at San Antonio

Inocoplo Indians entered the San Antonio de Valero Mission

Postito Indians reported at San José Mission

Negro slaves in Texas numbered forty-one

1786

August 17. David Crockett born in northwestern Tennessee

1787

Souanetto Indians reported in Texas by Henri Joutel

1790

The Nacisi Indians moved from Louisiana into Texas

Salapaque Indians reported at San Antonio

1793

Nuestra Señora del Refugio Mission established as the last of the Texas missions

March 2. Sam Houston born in Rockbridge County, Virginia

November 3. Stephen F. Austin born in southwestern Virginia

1794

Brazos Largos, Gumpusa, Parantone, and Prieto Indians reported near Goliad

Parantone and Vende Indians reported at Nuestra Señora del Espíritu Santo de Zuñiga Mission

1795

A group of Pawnee Indians visited San Antonio

James Bowie born in Tennessee

1796

Tawakoni Indians asked for a mission but were refused by the Spanish

1798

House of Barr and Davenport organized in Natchitoches, Louisiana, to trade in Texas

August 16. Mirabeau Buonaparte Lamar born in Louisville, Georgia

1800

Tenicapeme Indians reported in South Texas

1801

Tanima Indians reported in Texas

1805

Major village of the Orcoquiza Indians located on the Colorado River

Pakana Indians reported in East Texas

September 28. Port of San Bernard (Bernardo) established on the Texas coast by royal decree from Spain

October. Manuel Antonio Cordéro y Bustamante became governor of Texas

1806

April. Freeman's Red River Expedition, led by Thomas Freeman, to explore portions of the Louisiana Purchase, began

November 6. General James Wilkinson and Lieutenant Colonel Simón de Herrera agreed upon the Neutral Ground Agreement to settle the boundary dispute between Louisiana and Texas

1807

Toboso Indians reported at Nuestra Señora del Refugio Mission

1809

August 9. William Barret Travis born in South Carolina ·

1811

The Casas Revolution began in San Antonio led by Juan Bautista de las Casas

July. Simón de Herrera named *ad interim* governor of Texas

August 3. Juan Bautista de las Casas executed in Monclova and the Casas Revolution ended

1812

The Gaines House built on the west bank of the Sabine River and was the first house encountered in Texas for persons coming from Louisiana

August 8. The Gutiérrez-Magee Expedition entered Texas

1813

Trammel's Trace from Arkansas to Texas blazed by Nicholas Trammel

March 29. Battle of Rosalis (also known as the battle of Rosillo and as the battle of Salado) fought near the confluence of Salado Creek and the San Antonio River

May 29. *Gaceta de Tejas,* the first newspaper for Texas, published

June. *El Mejicano* published in Natchitoches, Louisiana, and circulated in Texas

August 18. Battle of the Medina River fought between forces of the Gutiérrez-Magee Expedition and a Spanish royalist force under Joaquín de Arredondo

1816

The following Indian tribes reported in Texas by Henry Ker: Ilisee (on the Red River), Obodeus (on the upper Red River), Parathee (in northwest Texas)

1817

The first Methodist minister and first Protestant to arrive in Texas, William Stevenson, arrived in present Red River County

1818

A group of Polish veterans arrived in Texas and settled near present Liberty

1819

February 22. The Adams-Oñis Treaty signed that established the western boundary of Louisiana Purchase and the eastern boundary of Texas

June 8. An advance force of the Long Expedition, led by Eli Harris, entered Texas across the Sabine River

August 14. *Texas Republican* began publication at Nacogdoches

1820

Delaware Indians moved into Texas for the first time

1821

Louis and Henry Rueg moved to Nacogdoches and were probably the first Swiss in Texas

Samuel Isaacks, the first recorded Jewish settler in Texas, came with Stephen F. Austin

Robbin's Ferry established in Madison County

January 17. Grant for Moses Austin to settle 300 families in Texas approved

June 10. Moses Austin died before being able to settle his colony in Texas

November. Fort Bend built near present site of Richmond in a big bend of the Brazos River

November. The schooner, *The Lively,* left New Orleans with colonists for Texas

1822

October 21. The Banco Nacional de Tejas, the first national bank in Texas, established in San Antonio by order of Governor José Felix Trespalacios

1823

April 9. The prospectus issued for a bilingual newspaper in San Antonio to be called the *Texas Courier*

1824

April 8. Martín de León petitioned Mexican government for permission to found a colony in Texas

August. A constituent congress assembled at Saltillo to write a constitution for the state of Coahuila and Texas

September. Battle of Jones Creek fought between Texans and Karankawa Indians

1825

The earliest known Scots came to Texas

What is believed to be the first sawmill in Texas built near San Augustine

April 15. Contract given to Haden Edwards to settle residents in Texas that became known as the Edwards Colony

April 15. Grant for DeWitt's Colony led by Green C. DeWitt approved

1826

Eagle Island Plantation established in Brazoria County
One of the first mills propelled by water built on Mill Creek by James, John, and William Cummings
December 16. The Fredonian Rebellion began when the Republic of Fredonia was proclaimed in Nacogdoches

1827

March 11. Constitution of Coahuila and Texas adopted

1828

Moore's Fort built near La Grange by John Henry Moore
The McMullen-McGloin Colony founded at present San Patricio
James Bowie came to Texas
Some of the Garza Indians reported living near Mier
A group of Quapaw Indians reported living in Texas
February 11. Freemasonry began in Texas when several York Rite Masons considered organizing a lodge in Texas

1829

First attempt to produce sugar in Texas made at Stephen F. Austin's colony
Sumner Bacon came as the first Cumberland Presbyterian to Texas
First Sunday School established by Thomas J. Pilgrim, a Baptist, at Sealy, Texas
March 12. Grant to settle families in Texas given to Lorenzo de Zavala
June. The first steamship used in Texas, the *Ariel*, arrived at the mouth of the Rio Grande
September 4. The *Mexican Advocate*, a bilingual newspaper, began publication at Nacogdoches
September 15. The Guerrero Decree abolishing slavery in the Republic of Mexico issued by Vicente Guerrero
September 25. *Texas Gazette* began publication at San Felipe de Austin

1830

José Luis Carvajal obtained the property at a crossing on Cibolo Creek in Karnes County, and it became known as Carvajal Crossing
James Bowie obtained a charter for the Coahuila Manufacturing

THE SOCORRO MISSION in 1930 from the Calleros Estate, El Paso, Texas.
— *Photo from The University of Texas Institute of Texan Cultures.*

Company from the Mexican government to establish a cotton mill for textile production

The San Patricio Trail established by the Irish between San Patricio and San Antonio

Thompson's Ferry began operation over the Brazos River near Richmond in Fort Bend County

April 6. The Law of April 6, 1830, initiated to stop American immigration into Texas and became a stimulus to the Texas Revolution

October 16. The Galveston Bay and Texas Land Company organized in New York to colonize Texas

October 17. Fort Tenoxtitlán, designed to stop immigration in Texas, established in Burleson County

November 1. The Precinct of Viesca created as a subdivision of the Mexican government

1831

Fort Anahuac on Galveston Island built

January. The *Mexican Citizen* began publication at San Felipe de Austin

October 1. Fort Terán, named for Manuel de Mier y Terán, established in Tyler County

1832

Committees of Safety and Correspondence, similar to those in the American Revolution, created in Texas

March. *Texas Gazette and Brazoria Commercial Advertiser* began publication at Brazoria

Summer. The expedition of José Antonio Mexia began

June 13. The Turtle Bayou Resolutions approved pledging the Texans to support constitutional government

June 26. Battle of Velasco, probably the first case of bloodshed between Texas and Mexico, occurred

August. *Constitutional Advocate and Brazoria Advertiser* began publication at Brazoria

August 2. Battle of Nacogdoches began

October 1. The Convention of 1832 met to ask for governmental reforms from Mexico

December. The family of James Franklin Perry arrived at Peach Point Plantation near Brazoria

1833

Groce's Retreat, a plantation, built in Grimes County

March 9. Capital of the state of Coahuila and Texas moved from Saltillo to Monclova

April 1. The Convention of 1833 met to correct weaknesses in the Convention of 1832

July. First Methodist class organized at McMahan's Chapel in Sabine County and began the first Protestant Church organized in Texas

November 11. Members of the Beales' Rio Grande Colony embarked from New York on the *Amos Wright*

November 23. Earliest known issue of *Advocate of the People's Rights* published in Brazoria

1834

Trade relations opened between Kiowa Indians and Americans

McKinney, Williams and Company, the largest commission-merchant firm in early Texas, founded at Quintana

Henry Stephenson appointed to the Texas Mission as the first Methodist preacher appointed to Texas

Fort Parker established in present Limestone County to protect the family of John Parker

January. Colonel Juan N. Almonte dispatched to Texas to make an inspection and to promise governmental reforms

January 28, February 8. O.P.Q. Letters written anonymously by Anthony Butler in an attempt to get Texas colonists to protest the imprisonment of Stephen F. Austin

February. Thomas Jefferson Chambers made state attorney of the state of Coahuila and Texas

March 12. The Beales' Rio Grande Colony was established and named "Delores"

July 5. *Texas Republican* began publication at Brazoria

1835

Fort Sullivan established in Milam County by Augustus W. Sullivan as a trading post

Juan N. Almonte reported the Kickapoo Indians living near Nacogdoches

Pecan Point Plantation in Red River County bought by Robert Hamilton

Lacy's Fort built near Alto in Cherokee County

Liberty Volunteers, organized by Andrew Briscoe at Harrisburg, joined the Texas Army

The Morgan Lines, first steamship company in Texas, began operation

Shawnee Indians reported in Texas by Juan N. Almonte

Thomas Jefferson Green arrived in Texas as head of the Texas Land Company, but nothing ever came of it

Spring. Fort Houston, named for Sam Houston, completed in Anderson County

June 29-30. Disturbance at Anahuac between Texan and Mexican forces

September. Martín Perfecto de Cós sent to Texas to investigate reasons for the Anahuac Disturbances

September 27. Francisco Castañeda, a lieutenant in the Mexican army, sent to retrieve a cannon loaned earlier to the citizens of Gonzales

October. The Permanent Council appointed a special committee to establish mail routes and named John Rice Jones as postmaster general

October. B.J. White reported an attempted slave revolt on the Brazos River

October 2. The Battle of Gonzales fought on Guadalupe River

October 10. *Telegraph and Texas Register* begun at San Felipe de Austin

October 11. The Permanent Council began governing Texas, but it lasted for only three weeks

October 13. New Orleans Greys organized in New Orleans to fight in the Texas Revolution

October 16. The Consultation met at San Felipe de Austin to consider a Texas response to the dictatorship of Antonio López de Santa Anna

October 17. Resolution offered by Daniel Parker to create the Texas Rangers

October 28. The battle of Concepción fought near San Antonio

October 28. The Old Mill in San Antonio became headquarters of Texas army under Stephen F. Austin

October 31. Detachment of the Lipantitlán Expedition left Goliad led by Ira Westover

November. The Red Rovers organized at Courtland, Alabama, to fight in the Texas Revolution

November. Mobile Grays organized in Mobile, Alabama, to fight in the Texas Revolution

November. *Texian and Emigrant's Guide* began publication at Nacogdoches

November 4. Fort Lipantitlán captured from Mexican forces by Texas volunteers

November 7. The decision of the Consultation to stay with the Mexican government and fight for restoration of constitutional government announced in the Declaration of November 7, 1835

November 14. The General Council began its sessions governing Texas

23

November 25. General Council passed a bill providing for the establishment of the Texas Navy

November 26. The Grass Fight, a part of the siege of Bexar, occurred

December. The Kentucky Mustangs, a volunteer force of Kentucky and Tennessee immigrants, formed in Nacogdoches

December 5. Siege of Bexar began

December 9. The area later to be known as Fort San Jacinto, named for the battle of San Jacinto, on Galveston Island reserved for public purposes

December 20. The Goliad Declaration of Independence read and approved

December 25. The Georgia Battalion entered the service of Texas in the Revolutionary War

December 27. Fort Milam established in Falls County

December 27. First Masonic lodge formed in Texas

December 31. The steamboat, *Yellow Stone,* left New Orleans to transport volunteers to Texas

1836

Buckeye Rangers, a volunteer company, was recruited for the Texas Revolution near Cincinnati, Ohio, by James L. Allen and an organization known as the Friends of Texas

A volunteer ranger group known as the Horse Marines organized

The Mansion House, a hotel, built in San Augustine

The *Thomas Toby* commissioned as a privateer in the Texas Navy

Fort Travis, named for William B. Travis, established on Galveston Island

The two cannon known as the "Twin Sisters" sent to aid Texan independence by citizens of Cincinnati, Ohio

The name of whip-handle dispatch given to a group of letters sent from Mexico to Texas hidden in a hollow whip handle

The following counties were created: Austin, named for Stephen F. Austin; Bastrop, named for Baron Felipe Enrique Neri de Bastrop; Colorado, named for the Colorado River; Goliad, named for the town of Goliad; Gonzales, named for Rafael Gonzales; Harrisburg, named for the municipality of Harrisburg; Jefferson, named for Thomas Jefferson; Liberty; Matagorda, named for the dense cane in the area; Milam, named for Benjamin R. Milam; Nacogdoches, named for the town which was named for the local Indians; Red River, named for the river; Refugio, named for the municipality of Refugio; San Augustine, named for the municipality of San Augustine; San Patricio; Shelby, named for Isaac Shelby; Victoria, named for the town which was a

24

shortened version of Nuestra Señora de Guadalupe de Jesús Victoria; Washington, named for Washington-on-the-Brazos

January. The General Council issued orders for an expedition against Matamoros to be led by Francis W. Johnson and James W. Fannin, Jr.

January. The *Independence* became the flagship of the Texas Navy

January. The schooner, *William Robbins,* purchased for the Texas Navy and rechristened the *Liberty*

January 14. The Runaway Scrape of the Texas Revolution began

January 18. The schooner *Invincible* purchased for the Texas Navy

January 19. The Red Rovers volunteer soldiers arrived in Texas

January 25. The schooner, *Brutus,* sold by John K. and Augustus C. Allen to the Texas Navy

February. La Bahía Presidio (Nuestra Señora de Loreto) renamed Fort Defiance by James W. Fannin, Jr

February. The expedition to Matamoros attacked at San Patricio where all but five were killed

February 1. Delegates elected to what became known as the Convention of 1836 that wrote the Declaration of Independence and the constitution of the Republic, organized the *ad interim* government, and named Sam Houston commander-in-chief

February 12. Committee of Vigilance and Safety of San Augustine authorized Haden Edwards to solicit donations from women in the United States to raise a "Ladies Battalion"

February 12. Mobile Grays became a part of the Texas Army under James W. Fannin, Jr.

February 23. Sam Houston signed a peace treaty with Cherokee Indians

February 23. General Antonio López de Santa Anna and the first of his troops arrived in San Antonio

February 24. The siege of the Alamo began

February 26. Colt revolver patented

February 27. Battle of San Patricio fought near San Patricio

Spring. The *Flash*, a privateer, fitted out for Texas use

March 1. Convention of 1836 met at Washington-on-the-Brazos

March 2. Battle of Agua Dulce Creek fought

March 2. Declaration of Independence of the Republic of Texas adopted

March 6. James Bowie killed at battle of the Alamo

March 6. The siege of the Alamo ended and it fell to the forces of Santa Anna

March 11. Sam Houston took command of the Texas army

March 14. The Battle of Refugio occurred during the Texas Revolution

March 16. The *ad interim* government of the Republic of Texas established

March 16. David G. Burnet elected president of the *ad interim* government of Texas

March 17. The following counties were created: Jackson, named for Andrew Jackson; Jasper, named for William Jasper; Mina, created from the municipality of Mina (later became Bastrop County)

March 19-20. Battle of Coleto occurred as the culmination of the Goliad campaign

March 20. Texas schooner *Invincible* captured the American brig *Pocket* off the Texas coast

March 27. Goliad Massacre occurred

April 1. Samuel Price Carson sent to Washington, D.C. to represent Texas interests

April 21. Battle of San Jacinto resulted in Texas independence

May. Toby and Brother Company of New Orleans became the purchasing agent for the Republic of Texas

May 14. Two treaties of Velasco signed by *ad interim* President David G. Burnet and General Antonio López de Santa Anna

May 19. Fort Parker attacked by Comanche and Caddo Indians and Cynthia Ann Parker was taken captive

June. The *Ocean*, a steamboat of the Texas Navy, was in use at Velasco

June. Fort Colorado established near Austin as a Texas Ranger fort

June 6. Buckeye Rangers left Cincinnati, Ohio, to participate in Texas Revolution

July. Antonio López de Santa Anna held prisoner at Orozimbo Planation in present Brazoria County

July 21. Texan forces began blockade of Matamoros that lasted until November 1, 1836

September. Texans voted overwhelmingly to seek annexation to the United States

October. First seat of government of Republic of Texas established at Columbia

October 3. First Congress of the Republic of Texas convened at Columbia

October 16. Sam Houston installed as President of the Republic of Texas

December. The Neches River Boundary Claim settled by achieving of Texas independence

December. Camp Independence in Jackson County occupied by army of the Texas Republic

December. Stephen F. Austin and other Texas commissioners designed a flag for Texas

December 10. David White appointed agent of the Texas Republic at Mobile, Alabama

December 10. First official flag of the Republic of Texas, known as David G. Burnet's flag, adopted

December 10. Texas Congress authorized the issuance of land scrip to be sold in the United States, the proceeds to be applied to the public debt

December 15. President Sam Houston ordered government of Texas moved to Houston

December 16. Texas Railroad, Navigation, and Banking Company chartered

December 20. Post Office Department of the Republic of Texas formally created

December 20. Congress of the Republic of Texas passed a law regulating ferries

December 20. Bexar County, named for the Department of Bexar, and Brazoria County, named for the Brazos River, created

December 22. General Land Office established by the Texas Congress

December 27. Stephen F. Austin died at age 43

December 29. Texas Senate tabled the treaty negotiated earlier by Sam Houston with the Cherokee Indians

1837

Texas Steam Mill Company chartered in Harris County

The O6 brand registered in Calhoun County for the Kokernot Ranch

First Cumberland Presbytery organized in Texas

First Baptist Church in Texas established at Washington-on-the-Brazos by Z. N. Morrell

Fort Fisher established at Waco Springs as a temporary Texas Ranger post

Austin, Bastrop, Colorado, Goliad, Gonzales, San Augustine, San Patricio, Shelby, and Victoria counties organized

The following counties were created: Fayette, named for the Marquis de Lafayette; Fort Bend, named for old Fort Bend; Houston, named for Sam Houston, Montgomery, named for General Richard Montgomery; Robertson, named for Sterling C. Robertson

January. Harrisburg County (now Harris County), named for John Richardson Harris, organized

January 26. The *Laura*, the first seafaring ship to penetrate Buffalo Bayou, reached Houston

February 5. Albert Sidney Johnston and Felix Huston fought a duel near Camp Independence

Spring. A desire to attack Matamoros again by General Felix Huston stopped by President Sam Houston

March. Velasco *Herald* began publication at Velasco

March 17. Fort Inglish established by Bailey Inglish in Fannin County

April. President Sam Houston named Nathaniel Townsend consul to New Orleans

April 19. Capital of Texas established at Houston

May 5. Captain Henry Teal assassinated at Camp Independence

June. *Texas Chronicle* began publication at Nacogdoches

June 5. Independence Academy chartered in Washington County

June 5. The University of San Augustine chartered

August 2. Matagorda *Bulletin* began publication

August 3. The *Eliza Russell* captured by Texas vessels in the Gulf of Mexico and taken to Galveston

August 4. Subject of Texas annexation formally presented to the United States

November. The *Single Star* began publication at Brazoria

November 20. Secretary of State R. A. Irion recommended that the Republic grant patents

December 5. The Philosophical Society of Texas founded at Houston

December 14. Sabine County, named for the municipality of Sabine, created

December 14. Fannin County, named for James Walker Fannin, Jr., created

December 14. Board of Medical Censors created to grant licenses to practice medicine and surgery

December 15. Joint resolution of Texas Congress passed concerning the formation of a consular service

December 16. Texas Senate declared null and void the treaty negotiated in 1836 by Sam Houston with Cherokee Indians

December 18. Name of Mina County changed to Bastrop County

1838

Fayette and Robertson counties organized

Galveston County, named for Count Bernardo de Gálvez, created

The first novel written in English in Texas, *Mexico vs. Texas*, published anonymously in Philadelphia

McKinney, Williams and Company moved from Quintana to Galveston

The New Washington Association headed by Samuel Swartwout formed to purchase Texas land

Merchant brig *Potomac* purchased for the Texas Navy

Customhouse built at the Port of Sabine

Stephenson's Ferry established on the Sulphur River in Bowie County by Joseph A. Stephenson

Swedish settlement in Texas begun with the arrival of S.M. Swenson at Houston

The theatre organization, "Thespian Corps," organized at San Augustine

January. Britain filed claims against Republic of Texas for destruction of the ship, *Little Penn*

January. The *National Intelligencer* published at Houston

February. *The People* began publication at Brazoria

Spring. Fannin County organized

March 9. Milam Guards commissioned by President Sam Houston as a police force and frontier guard

April 25. The *National Banner* began publication in Houston by J. Warren Niles

May 8. *The Civilian* began publication at Houston but moved to Galveston shortly thereafter

May 24. Brazos and Galveston Railroad Company chartered

Summer. The *Gazette* published at Richmond

Summer. *Commercial Intelligencer,* said to be the first Galveston newspaper, began publication

June 11. A theatre opened in Houston, probably the first in Texas

August 7. Cordova Rebellion began led by Vicente Cordova

September. *The Civilian* began publication at Galveston

September. The *Red-Lander* began publication at San Augustine

September 25. First missionary to Texas, Caleb Semper Ives, appointed by the Protestant Episcopal Church

October 2. On instructions of President Sam Houston, the offer of Texas annexation to the United States was withdrawn

October 8. Battle Creek Fight between surveyors and Kickapoo Indians occurred in Navarro County

November 10. David G. Burnet elected vice president of the Republic of Texas along with Mirabeau B. Lamar as president

December. Fort Sherman established in present Titus County

December 21. A Military Road was projected for the Republic of Texas by an act of the Texas Congress

December 31. President Mirabeau B. Lamar of the Republic of Texas urged the organization of a National Bank of Texas

1839

The first hotel in Austin, the Bullock House, built

"Cherokee War" occurred between white settlers in northeast Texas and Cherokee, Kickapoo, and Shawnee Indians

FOUR TIGUA Indian scouts.
— *Photo from The University of Texas Institute of Texan Cultures, John Davis.*

The Chihuahua Trail opened

Fort Crawford built by W.C. Crawford in Harrison County

Kenney's Fort built in present Williamson County

Regulator-Moderator War began in Shelby, Panola, and Harrison counties

Half-interest in Retrieve Plantation in Brazoria County sold to James Hamilton

Rutersville College created by the Texas Conference of the Methodist Church

Tahocullake Indians expelled from Texas along with the Cherokees

January 23. Texas Senate approved of President Sam Houston's withdrawal of offer of Texas annexation to the United States

January 24. Texas State Library established by the Congress of the Republic of Texas

January 25. President Mirabeau B. Lamar signed law adopting a new flag for the Republic of Texas

January 25. Coat of arms of the Republic of Texas officially adopted

January 26. Texas Congress passed a Texas Homestead Law

January 27. Caleb Semper Ives organized Christ Church, Matagorda, the first Episcopal Church in Texas

January 28. Harrison County, named for Jonas Harrison, created and organized

January 28. Patent office for the Republic of Texas within the department of state approved by President Mirabeau B. Lamar

February 17. The *Brazos Courier* began publication in Brazoria by R.L. Weir

Spring. Battle of Brushy Creek (also called battle of the Cottonwoods) occurred near Taylor

March 20. The *Galvestonian* began publication

March 23. The sidewheeler *Zavala* commissioned in the Texas Navy

April 8. The *Morning Star* began publication in Houston

April 27. The Richmond *Telescope* began publication

May 15-17. Battle of the San Gabriels occurred

May 16. *Colorado Gazette and Advertiser* began publication at Matagorda

May 26. Bird's Creek Indian Fight occurred near Temple

June. The schooner *San Jacinto* commissioned in the Texas Navy

June 3. Name of the Richmond *Telescope* changed to *The Richmond Telescope and Texas Miscellaneous Register*

June 12. Publisher of *The Richmond Telescope and Texas Miscellaneous Register* called it the *Richmond Telescope and Texas Literary Register*

July 6. The *Texas Emigrant* first published at Washington-on-the-Brazos by J. Warren Niles

July 15-16. The battle of the Neches fought as the principal engagement of the Cherokee War

July 16. Chief Bowles killed at the Battle of the Neches

August. The Webster Massacre by Comanche Indians occurred in Williamson County

August 1. First lots sold in what became Austin, Texas

August 7. The schooner *San Antonio* commissioned in the Texas Navy

August 26. Fort Burleson, named for Edward Burleson, established in present Falls County

August 31. The schooner *San Bernard* arrived in Galveston to be commissioned in the Texas Navy

September 29. Treaty signed between France and Texas in which France recognized Texas independence and accepted Texas commerce

October 3. Battle of Alcantra in Mexico in which 180 Texans participated

October 18. The brig *Wharton* arrived in Texas to become a part of the Texas Navy

October 30. The *City Gazette*, the first newspaper published in Austin, made its first appearance

December 14. Texas Congress passed a law providing for the building of a National Road

December 28. Name of Harrisburg County changed to Harris County

1840

The following counties created: Bowie, named for James Bowie; Lamar, named for Mirabeau B. Lamar; Travis, named for William Barret Travis

Fort Boggy, named for Boggy Creek, built in Leon County

Fort Johnson, named for Francis W. Johnson, established in Grayson County

Clarksville Female Academy (also called Mrs. Weatherred's School) opened near Clarksville

January 5. The flagship of the Texas Navy, the *Austin*, was commissioned

January 15. *Texas Sentinel* began publication at Austin

January 17. A convention in Laredo declared independence for the Republic of the Rio Grande in an effort to break away from the central government in Mexico

January 19. Site of Texas capital established in Austin

January 28. The first chamber of commerce in Texas founded in Houston

February 1. Rutersville College opened near La Grange

February 4. Union Academy chartered near Washington-on-the-Brazos

February 5. Trinity County, originally called the Northern Division of Liberty County, created for judicial purposes

February 14. The Austin Lyceum organized

February 14. Commercial treaty made between France and the Republic of Texas

February 21. Travis County organized

March 1. Travis Guards organized in Austin for home protection and campaigns against Indians

March 4. *Daily Times* began publication in Houston

March 19. Council House Fight occurred in San Antonio

April. *Daily Courier* began publication in Galveston

April 2. *Weekly Times* began publication in Houston

April 20. The sloop-of-war *Texas* was renamed *Austin*

April 25. The brig built as the *Galveston of Baltimore* but renamed the *Archer* arrived in Texas to join the Texas Navy, but it was never used

May. Camp Cazneau established in Williamson County to search for Comanches

May 28. The *Journal and Advertiser* began publication at San Augustine

June. The *Spy* was being published in Austin

June. The *Six-Pounder* was being published in Austin

July 13. The *Musquito* began publication in Houston

August 8. Linnville in Calhoun County sacked and burned by Comanches

August 11. The Plum Creek Fight occurred near present Lockhart

September 1. The *San Luis Advocate* began publication at San Luis

September 15. James Hamilton signed a treaty of commerce for the Republic of Texas with Holland

November 14. The Anglo-Texan Convention agreed to between Texas and England but refused by Mexico

1841

Roman Catholic population of Texas estimated to be 10,000

John M. Odin appointed Roman Catholic vicar-apostolic of Texas

First Church of the Disciples of Christ (Christian Church) founded in Texas in Bowie County

First settler in Dallas, John Neely Bryan, established himself near present courthouse square

Rumors of slave rebellions around Nacogdoches caused harsh measures to be taken

Gibbs Brothers & Company, supposedly the oldest continuous business in Texas on its original site and under the same ownership, began at Huntsville

Johannes Norbdoe, the first known Norwegian settler in Texas, settled near Dallas

Morning Herald began publication in Galveston

The *Journal and Advertiser* and the *Red-Lander* of San Augustine merged under the name, *Red-Lander*

Bird's Fort established north of present Arlington

Texas Baptist Education Society established

McKenzie College opened near Clarksville

Navasota County (later Brazos County) created

Tyler County, named for President John Tyler, created, but organization was abandoned after a few months

January 9. Harrisburg and Brazos Railroad chartered

January 12. The Franco-Texienne Bill introduced in Texas Congress to allow French colonization in Texas

January 13. Republic of Texas granted the church of the Alamo to the Roman Catholic Church

January 15. Houston and Austin Turnpike Company chartered

January 19. Ward County created for judicial purposes

January 21. Spring Creek County created for judicial purposes

January 22. Menard County created for judicial purposes, but was declared unconstitutional in 1842

January 28. Paschal County created for judicial purposes

January 29. Neches County created for judicial purposes

January 30. Burnet County created as a judicial county

January 30. Galveston University chartered by the Texas Congress

January 30. Panola County created for judicial purposes

January 30. Guadalupe College chartered in Gonzales

February. Lamar County organized

February 3. Companies of volunteer minutemen authorized by the Texas Congress for protection against Indians

February 7. Bethel Baptist Church organized in Sabine County

March. *The Rambler* began publication in Austin

March. The *Houstonian* began publication

April. The *Tarantula* began publication at Washington-on-the-Brazos

April 21. Alphonse de Saligny purchased land in Austin for the French Embassy

April 22. Name of *Texas Sentinel* changed to *Texas Centinel*

May. Diplomatic relations between France and Texas were broken off because of the so-called Pig War

May 12. The *People's Advocate* began publication at Galveston

May 24. Battle of Village Creek occurred in Tarrant County between Indians and Texas Rangers

Summer. San Patricio Minute Men organized at San Patricio to provide defense against an expected Mexican invasion

June 8. "Port of Houston" established by city government of Houston

June 19. The Texan Santa Fe Expedition set out to Santa Fe to occupy the Texas claim to New Mexico

August. The *National Intelligencer* published at Galveston by A.J. Cody

September 6. Edward Burleson elected vice president of the Republic of Texas

November. *Weekly Texian* began publication at Austin

November 1. *Daily Advertiser* began publication in Galveston

November 27. *Daily Bulletin* began publication in Austin

December. The *Daily Texian* began publication in Austin

December 7. Name of Northern Division of Liberty County changed to Trinity County (a judicial county)

December 13. David G. Burnet became President of the Republic of Texas when Mirabeau B. Lamar resigned

1842

The *Brazos Farmer* began publication at Washington-on-the-Brazos

Clarksville Academy opened in Red River County

The *Croaker,* a Galveston newspaper, made its first appearance

Navasota County, created in 1841, was renamed Brazos County after the Brazos River

Texas Supreme Court decision in Stockton *v.* Montgomery declared judicial counties unconstitutional

Second Battle of Bandera Pass fought

The judicial county of Waco created but abolished the same year

The Order of San Jacinto created by Sam Houston to honor distinguished Texans

January 9. General Mariano Arista warned Texans from Monterrey that their plans for independence were futile and that a Mexican invastion was on its way

January 15. Burleson County as a judicial district was formed

January 18. Marshall University chartered at Marshall

January 29. La Baca, Guadalupe, and Waco counties created for judicial purposes but abolished in 1842 when judicial counties were declared unconstitutional

February 1. Smith County created for judicial purposes

February 2. De Witt, Hamilton and Madison counties created for judicial purposes but were abolished by a Texas Supreme Court decision

February 15. Henri Castro received two grants of land on which he was to settle six hundred families

March. The newspaper, the *Anti-Quaker*, published in Austin

March 5. Mexican troops under Rafael Vásquez arrived at San Antonio in an invasion of Texas

March 10. Beginning of the "Archive War" between Austin and Houston over the control of the Texas State Archives

March 13. President Sam Houston, fearing Mexican attack, ordered the seat of government moved to Houston

April. Diplomatic relations resumed between France and Texas after the Pig War

April 11. Galveston *News* began publication

April 20. The Adelsverein or Association of Noblemen organized in Germany to purchase land for settlement in Texas

May. The *Sabine Advocate* began publication at Pulaski

Summer. The *Montezuma* affair occurred between Texas and England

June. *Texian and Brazos Farmer* began publication after combining the *Weekly Texian* of Austin and the *Brazos Farmer* of Washington-on-the-Brazos

June 7. Fisher-Miller Land Grant given by Republic of Texas to settle Europeans in Texas

July. Antonio Canales led a Mexican expedition into Texas which was defeated on the Nueces River

August. The *Commercial Chronicle,* a newspaper in Galveston, began publication

August 6. Charles Eliot arrived in Galveston as British chargé d' affaires to the Republic of Texas

August 16. The Warfield Expedition, led by Charles A. Warfield, set out for Santa Fe to retaliate for the capture of the Texan Santa Fe Expedition

August 20. The *Northern Standard,* owned by Charles DeMorse, began publication at Clarksville

September. Texas capital moved by executive order to Washington-on-the-Brazos

September 11. Mexican forces under General Adrian Woll captured San Antonio

September 18. Dawson Massacre occurred during the Mexican invasion of Texas

September 18. Battle of Salado began on Salado Creek near San Antonio

October 3. President Sam Houston ordered the Somervell Expedition organized by Alexander Somervell to invade Mexico if success seemed possible

October 12. *Texas Times* began publication at Galveston

November. The *Planter's Gazette* began publication at Columbia

December 19. The Mier Expedition began by selecting William S. Fisher as commander

1843

Brazos County organized

Rusk County, named for Thomas Jefferson Rusk, created

Kelly Plow Company, the only full line plow factory in the Southwest, began operation near Marshall

Name of *Commercial Chronicle* in Galveston changed to *Independent Chronicle*

The Cumberland Synod of Texas organized at Nacogdoches

January. The Marshall *Review* began publication

January 9. Nassau Farm in Fayette County owned by Robert Mills

January 28. Jacob Snively petitioned the government to organize a force to fight the Mexicans that eventually became the Snively Expedition

February 11. Mier Expedition captured in Mexico which led to the Black Bean Episode

February 18. The *Western Advocate* began publication at Austin

March 25. Members of the Mier Expedition were executed as a part of the Black Bean Episode

June. President Sam Houston agreed to an armistice with Mexico

June. The *Planter* began publication at Columbia

June. The *National Vindicator* established at Washington-on-the-Brazos

July 19. *The Citizen* (also called the *Weekly Citizen*) began publication at Houston

August. The *Independent Chronicle,* a successor of the *Commercial Chronicle,* began publication in Galveston

August 26. Cornerstone laid for the first building of Wesleyan Male and Female College at San Augustine

September. A Tehuacana Creek Council resulted in a treaty with the Waco and Caddo Indians

September 29. Edward H. Tarrant and George W. Terrell met with representatives of nine Indian tribes at Bird's Fort and signed a peace treaty

December. The *Weekly Dispatch* began publication at Matagorda

1844

Andrew Jackson Donelson appointed chargé d'affaires of the United States to the Republic of Texas

Ringwood Female Seminary opened at Boston, Texas

First Houston Academy opened in Houston

The *Literary Intelligencer* was being published at San Augustine under Methodist sponsorship

First Jewish cemetery established at Houston

Muleshoe Ranch and brand started in Red River County

January. *Texian Democrat* began publication at Houston

January 25. La Grange *Intelligencer* began publication at La Grange

January 27. Hermann's University chartered, but it never opened

January 29. President Sam Houston gave an empresario grant to Charles Fenton Mercer who established the Mercer colony

February. *Harrison Times* began publication at Marshall

February. *The Town* began publication at Galveston

February 5. The Texas Congress created a commission to build the Central National Road of the Republic of Texas

February 15. Name of Mansion hotel, a hotel in Houston, changed to DeChene's Hotel

April. A second Tehuacana Creek Council with the Indians called by President Sam Houston

April 7. The Verein (Association of German Noblemen) purchased a tract of land west of San Antonio

May 7. The river steamer *Scioto Bell* arrived at Galveston

June 8. Treaty to annex Texas rejected by the United States Senate

August 15. President Sam Houston called out the militia to put down the Regulator-Moderator War

October 9. At a Tehuacana Creek Council Sam Houston signed a treaty of peace with the Indians

December 7. *Texas National Register* began publication at Washington-on-the-Brazos

1845

The *Brazos Planter* at Brazoria began publication

Texas capital moved to Austin where it has remained permanently

Texas Cotton and Woolen Manufacturing Company chartered for textile production

First settlement of Norwegians in Texas made by Johan Reinert Reierson near present Brownsboro in Henderson County

Mary Hardin-Baylor College founded at Independence as a part of Baylor University

Glen Eden Plantation built in Grayson County by Holland Coffee

The term "maverick" came into use to designate unbranded cattle, named for Samuel A. Maverick

January 22. Republic of Texas enacted preemption law for persons residing on public land

February 1. Baylor University chartered by the Republic of Texas

February 1. Rusk County Academy incorporated at Henderson

February 3. Nacogdoches University chartered at Nacogdoches

February 3. Galveston Chamber of Commerce chartered

February 28. A joint resolution was adopted in the United States Congress offering statehood to Texas

March 14. The site of New Braunfels purchased by German settlers

April. Montgomery *Patriot* began publication at Montgomery

April 28. Cornerstone laid of what eventually became Sophienburg Museum at New Braunfels

July. The *New Era* began publication at Austin

July. *Texas State Paper* began publication at Galveston

July 4. Convention of 1845 met and approved annexation to the United States

August 15. Fort Marcy, named for William L. Marcy, established at Corpus Christi

September 15. La Grange Female Institute opened at La Grange

September 19. A third Tehuacana Creek Council met to consider treaties between Texas and local Indians

November. *Daily Globe* began publication in Galveston

November. The *Soda Lake Herald* began publication at Marshall

November 10. First group of Mormon settlers led by Lyman Wight arrived in Texas in Grayson County

December 29. Texas became a state of the United States

1846

The following counties were created: Anderson, named for Kenneth Lewis Anderson; Angelina, named for the Angelina River; Burleson, named for General Edward Burleson; Calhoun, named for John C. Calhoun; Cass, named for Lewis Cass of Michigan; Cherokee, named for the Cherokee Indians; De Witt, named for Green C. De Witt; Grayson, named for Peter W. Grayson; Henderson, named for James Pinckney Henderson; Hunt, named for Memucan Hunt; Lavaca, named for the Lavaca River; Leon, named for Martín de León and for a yellow wolf called the leon; Limestone, named for native limestone; Navarro, named for José Antonio Navarro; Nueces, named for the Nueces River; Smith, named for General James Smith; Tyler,

COMANCHE CHIEF QUANAH PARKER

created for the second time; Upshur, named for Abel Packer Upshur; Wharton, named for William H. and John A. Wharton

Texas Presbyterian began publication at Victoria

A **ferry** was established at Santa Margarita Crossing on the Nueces River near San Patricio

Masonic Collegiate Institute established at Anderson in Grimes County

Baylor University opened at Independence, Texas

Fort Leaton, named for its founder, Ben Leaton, established near present Presidio, Texas

Fort Smith, named for Major Thomas I. Smith, established in Hill County

January. Galveston *Beacon* began publication

January. A second *New Era* began publication at Austin

January 1. Corpus Christi *Gazette* began publication

January 9. Texas Literary Institute organized at Houston by the Convention of the Friends of Education

January 16. Wesleyan Male and Female College chartered at San Augustine

January 21. The *Texas Democrat* began publication at Austin

February. Thomas Jefferson Rusk and Sam Houston elected as first United States Senators from Texas

February 19. First state officials after annexation installed at Austin

February 19. Formal transfer of authority made from the Republic of Texas to the United States as statehood was achieved

March. Guadalupe County, named for the Guadalupe River, created

March. Taylor's Trail, followed by General Zachary Taylor, opened between the Nueces River and the Rio Grande

March 24. Comal County, named for the Comal River, created and organized

March 26. Fort Polk, named for President James K. Polk, established near Point Isabel in Cameron County

March 26. General Zachary Taylor and his forces of occupation arrived on the Rio Grande and established a military base that became Fort Brown, named for Major Jacob Brown

March 30. Dallas County, named for George M. Dallas, created

March 30. Panola County, named for the Indian word *ponolo* which means cotton, created

April 6. Grimes County, named for Jesse Grimes, created

April 6. Walker County, created and named originally for Robert J. Walker of Mississippi who supported Texas statehood but when he proved to be a Unionist the name was changed to honor Samuel H. Walker

April 11. Denton County, named for John B. Denton, created

April 11. Huntsville Academy at Huntsville, also known as the "Brick Academy," chartered

April 22. Newton County, named for Corporal John Newton, created

April 25. A skirmish between American and Mexican forces occurred near Brownsville, probably the first battle of the Mexican War

May. Titus County, named for Andrew J. Titus, created

May 8. The Battle of Palo Alto, first battle of the Mexican War, fought near Brownsville

May 8. Victoria *Advocate*, second oldest continuous newspaper in Texas, began publication at Victoria

May 9. Battle of Resaca de la Palma fought as second battle of the Mexican War

July. *Colorado Herald*, a weekly newspaper in Matagorda, started by James M. Dallam

July. Newton County organized

July 18. Walker County organized

August 9. Polk County, named for President James K. Polk, organized

1847

Evergreen Plantation on Galveston Bay purchased by Ashbel Smith

Forest Hill Plantation in Cherokee County developed

Morgan R. Smith became the sole owner of the Waldeck Plantation in Brazoria County

Fort Fitzhugh built in present Cooke County

Bettina, a small communistic community, established near Llano

The Commercial and Agricultural Bank at Galveston, the only bank chartered in Texas before the Civil War, opened

Texas raised to status of diocese in Roman Catholic Church and John M. Odin named the first bishop of Galveston

Texas Christian Advocate and Brenham Advertiser began as a Methodist newspaper

The original Nimitz Hotel built in Fredericksburg

Clarksville Male and Female Academy began as Clarksville Male Academy

Ursuline Academy established at Galveston

University of Eastern Texas organized at San Augustine

January 16. The Ursulines, the first order to come to Texas, came from New Orleans

January 19. The Ursuline Sisters, an Italian order, arrived at Galveston

February 13. The *Far West*, a newspaper in La Grange, began publication

March 2. The Meusebach-Comanche Treaty signed at San Sabá Presidio

1848

The following counties were created: Caldwell, named for Mathew Caldwell; Cameron, named for Ewen Cameron; Cooke, named for William G. Cooke; Gillespie, named for Captain Richard A. Gillespie; Kaufman, named for David Spangler Kaufman; Medina, named for the Medina River; Starr, named for James Harper Starr; Van Zandt, named for Isaac Van Zandt; Webb, named for James Webb

Clarksville Female Institute established in Red River County

McKenzie College chartered

Ringwood Female Seminary moved to Clarksville where it was called Clarksville Female Institute

Victoria Female Academy founded at Victoria under Presbyterian sponsorship

Term, "Free State of Van Zandt," came into usage

The Icarian Colony established by French immigrants near Fort Worth

Two cows and a bull from Queen Victoria's own herd of Durham cattle brought to Texas, the earliest recorded importation of purebred cattle

Baptist State Convention organized

Texas prison system established

February. Post of El Paso, now Fort Bliss, established

February 2. Treaty of Guadalupe Hidalgo which ended the Mexican War was signed

February 3. A group of about seventy men left France to establish the Icarian Colony in Texas

February 5. Guadalupe College chartered in Guadalupe City

March 1. Hays County, named for John Coffee Hays, created

March 10. Treaty of Guadalupe Hidalgo ratified by the United States Senate

March 11. Galveston and Red River Railroad (later Houston and Texas Central Railway Company) chartered

March 14. Williamson County, named for Major Robert M. Williamson, created

March 15. Santa Fe County, including the eastern half of the present state of New Mexico, created to press the claim of Texas to the Rio Grande as the western boundary of the state

March 16. Huntsville Male Institute chartered at Huntsville

March 18. Cherokee Academy at Rusk chartered

March 28. Milam Liberal Institute chartered at Cameron in Milam County

October. Colorado Female Academy opened in Austin

October 26. Fort Ringgold, named for Major David Ringgold, established in Starr County

November 20. Camp Austin on the Colorado River became a military depot

December. Hillyer Female College established at Goliad under Baptist sponsorship

December 5. Fort Martin Scott, named for Colonel Martin Scott, established near Fredericksburg

1849

Camp Eagle Pass on the Rio Grande abandoned when Fort Duncan was established

First Czechs settled in Texas at Cat Spring led by Josef Ernst Bergman

The Ford and Neighbors Trail between Austin and El Paso laid out

Fayetteville Academy opened at Fayetteville

Tarrant County, named for General E.H. Tarrant, created

The *State Gazette* began publication at Austin

Name of the *Texas Christian Advocate and Brenham Advertiser* changed to *Texas Wesleyan Banner*

Tohookatokie Indians reported in Texas

January 1. The Diocese of Texas of the Protestant Episcopal Church organized at Matagorda

February 14. *Texas Wesleyan Banner* established by the Methodist Church

Spring. La Grange Collegiate Institute opened at La Grange by Cumberland Presbyterian Church

March 3. Fort McIntosh, first named Camp Crawford for Secretary of War George W. Crawford, established near Laredo

March 13. Fort Inge, named for Lieutenant Zebulon M.P. Inge, established in Uvalde County

March 27. Fort Duncan established near Eagle Pass

March 27. Fort Graham, named for William M. Graham, established in the vicinity of present Hillsboro

March 30. *Texas Republican* began publication at Marshall

June 6. Fort Worth, named for Brigadier General William Jenkins Worth, established

July 7. Fort Lincoln, named for George Lincoln, established in Medina County

August. Henderson Female College opened in Henderson

September. Galveston Seminary opened

September 15. Camp San Elizario in El Paso County occupied by the United States Infantry

44

October 12. Fort Croghan, named for Colonel George Croghan, built in Burnet County

October 26. Fort Gates, named for Brevet Major Collinson Reed Gates, established near Gatesville

November 22. Austin College, affiliated with the Presbyterian Church, was incorporated at Huntsville

December 20. Ellis County, named for Richard Ellis, created

December 31. Guadalupe High School Association organized in Seguin

1850

The following counties were created: Freestone; Kinney, named for Henry L. Kinney; Trinity, named for the Trinity River; Uvalde, named for Captain Juan de Ugalde with the spelling altered; Wood, named for George T. Wood

Wyalucing Plantation home built at Marshall

Colony of Kent established in present Bosque County by the English Universal Immigration Company

Austin Female Academy opened

Washington Masonic School was in operation at Washington-on-the-Brazos

The Trube family, among the first Danes in Texas, arrived at Galveston

Senator Henry Stuart Foote of Mississippi proposed dividing Texas with a new state called San Jacinto, but it received little attention

First known attempt to grow rice in Texas

Tarrant County organized

Barlett-Condé Compromise effected concerning U.S.-Mexican boundary on the Rio Grande

Tenawa Indians had disappeared as a band by this time

Nacogdoches Archives transferred to the secretary of state's office

Bexar Manufacturing Company chartered for textile production

January. Santa Fe County divided into Worth, El Paso, Presidio, and Santa Fe counties

January 2. Texana Academy chartered at Texana in Jackson County

January 3. Worth County created out of Santa Fe County with Val Verde, New Mexico as the county seat

January 7. Name of Camp Crawford changed to Fort McIntosh in honor of Colonel J.B. McIntosh

January 22. Bell County, named for Peter H. Bell, created

January 22. McLennan County, named for Neil McLennan, created

45

January 26. Fowler Institute chartered at Henderson by the Methodist Episcopal Church

January 28. Falls County, named for the falls on the Brazos River, created

February 1. Act of Texas Legislature provided that Spanish and Mexican documents should be turned over to city councils

February 7. Charter for Chapel Hill College (also spelled Chappell Hill) granted to Marshall Presbytery of the Cumberland Presbyterian Church

February 8. Galveston and Brazos Navigation Company chartered to construct a canal near Galveston Bay

February 10. The Buffalo Bayou, Brazos, and Colorado Railway chartered as the first railroad in Texas

February 16. The women's division of Marshall University at Marshall turned over to the Marshall Masonic Lodge to establish the Masonic Female Institute

March. Fort Merrill, named for Captain Hamilton W. Merrill, established in Live Oak County

September. The Merchants War caused by Mexico's strict tariff laws began

September 4. Central Male and Female Institute chartered in Cass County

September 5. San Antonio and Mexican Gulf Railway chartered

September 5. Lockhart Academy incorporated at Lockhart

November. Camp Corpus Christi established

November 25. In compliance with the Compromise of 1850, Texas gave up all claims to the upper Rio Grande, present eastern New Mexico, and Santa Fe and Worth counties went out of existence

December 2. Masonic Female Institute chartered at Marshall

1851

Bastrop Academy opened its first session under jurisdiction of the Methodist Episcopal Church

Mount Enterprise Male and Female College opened by the Disciples of Christ in Rusk County

Stephens and Carter Academy established at Rusk

A second Ursuline Academy established, this one at San Antonio

Black's Fort established in Burnet County by William Black to protect local settlers

Camp Harney established in Zapata County as a temporary military base

B.H. Epperson was the candidate of the Whig Party in the governor's election

Mormon Mill Colony established near Burnet by survivors of the Zodiac settlement led by Lyman Wight

46

January. Freestone County organized

March 24. James Stephen Hogg, the first native governor of Texas, born near Rusk

June 24. Fort Belknap, named for its founder, General William G. Belknap, established

July 6. Fort Mason, named for Lieutenant George T. Mason or Brevet Brigadier General Richard Barnes Mason, established on Post Hill

August. A second organization known as the Travis Guards established at Austin for frontier defense

September. Masonic Institute of San Augustine began operation

November 1. Fort Belknap moved to a site in present Young County

November 14. Fort Phantom Hill, originally called Post on the Clear Fork of the Brazos, established near present Abilene

November 24. Jasper Collegiate Institute at Jasper chartered

1852

Fort Cienaga, a private fort, used for protection by Milton Favor

Camp Drum established at Zapata on the Rio Grande

Camp Merrill in Jim Wells County established on site formerly known as Camp Casa Blanca

Fort Moritas existed in Presidio County as a private fort for protection against Apache Indians

Kelly's Stage Stand operated in present Karnes County

Port Isabel Lighthouse built to guide commerce on the Rio Grande

The Alma Male and Female Institute founded at Hallettsville

The Austin Female Collegiate Institute opened

Johnson Institute founded in Hays County

Paris Female Institute founded at Paris, Texas

St. Mary's University, a Catholic institution in San Antonio, had its beginning

Tehuacana Academy was in operation under Presbyterian control at Tehuacana

Hidalgo County, named for Miguel Hidalgo y Costilla, created and organized

King Ranch had its beginning in Nueces County

A group of the Potawatomi Indians migrated to Texas

Battle of Hynes Bay fought between Texans and the Karankawa Indians

First Eastern Texas Railroad chartered

State Times established in Austin by John S. Ford and Joe Walker

January 1. St. Paul's College, an Episcopal school, opened at Anderson in Grimes County

January 5. Orange County, named for orange groves of George A. Patillo, created

February 2. Chapel Hill College opened at Daingerfield

February 5. Burnet County, named for David G. Burnet, created

February 5. Fort Terrett, named for Lieutenant John C. Terrett, established between present Junction and Sonora

February 9. Chappell Hill Male and Female Institute in Washington County chartered

February 13. Comal Union School in Comal County chartered

February 13. Richmond Male and Female Academy chartered at Richmond

February 16. Joint resolution introduced into the legislature to divide Texas into states of East Texas and West Texas, but measure failed

February 16. First of three railroads named the Texas Western Railroad chartered

February 16. Second of three railroads named the Texas Western Railroad chartered, but the second one was also captioned the Vicksburg and El Paso Railroad

February 16. Legislature authorized the governor to negotiate with the federal government for land for Indian reservations

February 16. Goliad College chartered near Goliad

February 16. Gonzales College chartered at Gonzales

March 2. Parker County organized

March 14. Fort McKavett (originally called Camp San Saba), named for Captain Henry McKavett, established in Menard County

March 15. Camp Joseph E. Johnston in Tom Green County occupied

May 18. Fort Ewell, named for Richard Stoddert Ewell, established in La Salle County

June 19. Fort Riley (later named Fort Clark), named for commanding officer of the 1st Infantry, established in present Kinney County

June 29. The first of the Sisters of the Incarnate Word and Blessed Sacrament, a French order, arrived in Galveston

July 15. Name of Fort Riley changed to Fort Clark in honor of Major John B. Clark

July 16. Beginning of the Hedgcoxe War, also known as the Peters' Colony Rebellion

October 28. Fort Chadbourne, named for Lieutenant Theodore L. Chadbourne, established in present Coke County

November 12. *Neu Braunfelser Zeitung,* first German language newspaper in Texas, began publication at New Braunfels

December. Paine Female Institute opened at Goliad as a Methodist institution

December 24. The "General Sherman," the first locomotive in Texas, placed in service at Harrisburg

1853

Paris Female Seminary started at Paris, Texas

Elisha M. Pease elected governor

William Leslie Cazneau appointed special agent to the Dominican Republic

Camp Elizabeth established as an outpost hospital of Fort Concho

Memphis, El Paso, and Pacific Railroad chartered

Mississippi and Pacific Railroad chartered

Hill County, named for George W. Hill, created and organized

Madison County, named for President James Madison, created

Largest of Norwegian settlements in Texas made in Bosque County by Ole Knutson

Tyler University founded at Tyler by the Cherokee Baptist Association

January. La Grange Preparatory School for Females opened in the buildings of La Grange Collegiate Institute

January. La Grange Male and Female Seminary and Boarding School opened at La Grange

January 17. Texas Medical Association organized at Austin

February. Live Oak Female Seminary opened near Brenham

February 7. Bastrop Academy, under the jurisdiction of the Methodist Epsicopal Church, chartered

February 7. Andrew Female College chartered at Huntsville under the jurisdiction of the Methodist Church

February 7. Cold Springs Female College incorporated in San Jacinto County

February 7. Galveston, Houston, and Henderson Railroad Company chartered

April 4. First session of Gonzales College opened

July 1. San Antonio *Zeitung,* the first German-language newspaper in San Antonio, began publication

September 2. Property donated in Rusk County for Church Hill Academy

September 7. Operation of Buffalo Bayou, Brazos, and Colorado Railway began

October 15-16. First organized song festival in Texas held at New Braunfels hosted by the Germania Singing Society

49

ANTONIO LÓPEZ de Santa Anna, Mexican President of Texas, drawn by Gene Bustamante.

From The Presidential Museum, Odessa, Texas — Photo by The University of Texas Institute of Texan Cultures.

Baylor University granted its first degree

Name of Clarksville Female Institute changed to Clarksville Male and Female Academy (originally Ringwood Female Seminary)

Eastern Texas Female College chartered at Tyler

Gilmer Female College, a Methodist institution, opened at Gilmer

Kaufman Masonic Institute established at Kaufman

Mound Prairie Institute organized near Palestine

Texas Military Institute founded in Galveston by Caleb G. Forshey

Alabama Indians moved to the Alabama-Coushatta Indian Reservation in Polk County

Koasati Indians went to the Alabama-Coushatta Indian Reservation

Brazos Indian Reservation established near present Graham by General Randolph B. Marcy

Anadarko Indians moved to the Brazos Indian Reservation

Hainai Indians placed on the Brazos Indian Reservation

Coryell County, named for James Coryell, organized

Karnes County, named for Henry W. Karnes, created

Fort Picketville established in Stephens County and named for either Bill Pickett or because the houses were made of pickets

The *Alamo Star* began publication in San Antonio

Texas Christian Advocate established at Galveston by the Methodist Episcopal Church, South

Know-Nothing Party, a secret organization, became politically active in Texas

First law regulating sale of alcoholic beverages passed by the legislature

Knights of the Golden Circle established as a secret organization to establish a strong slave empire

Earliest sulphur deposits to attract attention discovered

Name of Post of El Paso changed to Fort Bliss, named for Colonel William Wallace S. Bliss

January 5. Indian Creek Academy chartered in Jasper County, but it never opened

January 5. Texas and Red River Telegraph Company chartered

January 25. Aranama College at Goliad was granted a charter to educate Mexican youths under the jurisdiction of the Presbyterian Church

February. Bosque County, named for Bosque River, created

February 4. Galveston Wharf and Cotton Press Company chartered and given control of all waterfront facilities in Galveston

February 6. Bill passed setting aside land for Indian reservations in Texas

February 6. Law passed establishing the Brazos Indian Reservation for Caddo, Waco, Comanche, and other tribes

February 11. Chambers Terraqueous Transportation Company chartered to build 4,000 miles of road

February 11. Tyler University chartered at Tyler under Baptist sponsorship

February 13. Church Hill Academy in Rusk County incorporated

February 14. First telegraph office opened in Marshall by Texas and Red River Telegraph Company

February 14. The first Western Union Telegraph office in Texas opened at Marshall

February 18. Johnson County, named for Middleton Tate Johnson, created

March. Mormon settlement made on the Medina River across from the village of Bandera

March 23. San Antonio *Herald* began publication

May. Texas State Singing Society organized at San Antonio

May 3. Rio Grande Female Seminary organized by the Presbyterian Church

August. The Atlantic and Pacific Railroad Company purchased the charter of the Texas Western Railroad

August 7. Burnet County organized

September. A group of Wends left Germany for Texas where they established one of the two large colonies of Wends in the world

October 7. American soldiers arrived at a settlement named Painted Comanche Camp and established Fort Davis, named for Secretary of War Jefferson Davis

December 22. A party of recruits entered Texas on their way to start La Réunion, a French socialistic colony near Dallas

1855

Guadalupe Male and Female Academy opened on the site of the Guadalupe High School Association

Mound Prairie Institute opened

Shannon School opened in facilities used earlier by La Grange Preparatory School for Females and La Grange Collegiate Institute

Soule University established at Chappell Hill in Washington County by the Methodist Church

Camp Colorado located temporarily in Mills County

Governor's Mansion built in Austin

Elisha M. Pease reelected governor

Carrizo Indians raided from Mexico in the Brownsville area

Tanpacuaze Indians, known by the name Tampaquash, raided in the Brownsville area

Tonkawa Indians moved to the Brazos Indian Reservation

February 24. La Grange *Paper* began publication at La Grange

March 3. Congress passed the Shield Amendment authorizing funds to purchase camels for use in America

June 16. A group of settlers led by Dr. Augustin Savardan arrived at La Réunion

July 8. Camp Verde in Kerr County established as headquarters for the camel expedition

August 20. Fort Lancaster established in present Crockett County

August 30. First group of Comanches settled on Brazos Indian Reservation

October. The Callahan Expedition led by James Hughes Callahan was organized to protect Mexican border from Lipán-Apaches

December. Parker County, named for Isaac Parker, created

1856

The following counties were created: Atascosa, named for the Spanish word meaning boggy; Brown, named for Captain Henry S. Brown; Comanche, named for the Comanche Indians; Erath, named for George B. Erath; Jack, named for William H. and Patrick C. Jack; Live Oak, named for the live oak groves in the area; Maverick, named for Samuel A. Maverick; McCulloch, named for Ben McCulloch; Palo Pinto, named for the Palo Pinto River; Wise, named for Henry A. Wise; Young, named for Colonel William C. Young

The second Houston Academy chartered

Margaret Houston Female College chartered at Daingerfield in Cass County

New Braunfels Academy established at New Braunfels

Milam County established in its present form

Asylum for the Blind established in Austin

Texas School for the Deaf (originally called the Asylum for the Deaf and later the Deaf Institute) established

Uvalde County organized

The Old Land Office Building constructed in Austin

Planned slave rebellion exposed in Colorado County

Trinity River High School opened at Waco by the Baptist Church

Name of the Galveston and Red River Railroad changed to Houston and Texas Central Railway

Dallas incorporated as a town

January 3. Camp Cooper established in Throckmorton County by

53

Colonel Albert Sidney Johnston

January 15. Texas and New Orleans Telegraph Company chartered

January 18. Gilmer Female College chartered

January 25. Bandera County created

January 26. Kerr County, named for James Kerr, created

January 28. Henderson Female College chartered

February. Burleson Female Institute in Austin, conducted by Richard B. Burleson and sponsored by local Baptists, opened, but it closed before the end of the year

February 1. Encinal County created, but it was never organized

February 1. Lampasas County, named for the Lampasas River, created

February 1. San Saba County, named for the San Saba River, created

February 2. Soule University chartered

February 2. Washington County Railroad chartered

February 2. Franklin College chartered at Palestine in Anderson County

March. Luther Rice Baptist Female College projected at Marshall, but it never opened

March 10. Lampasas County organized

March 10. Bandera County organized

April 7. La Grange Select School opened as a school for girls in La Grange

April 9. Robert E. Lee arrived at Camp Cooper for an assignment of fifteen months

April 29. First camels arrived in Texas in a special experiment

May 13. The *Supply* arrived at Indianola with a cargo of camels

July 8. Camp Verde established

July 12. Camp Sabinal in Uvalde County established by Captain Albert G. Brackett to protect road from San Antonio to El Paso

July 29. The *Texas Monument* began publication in order to raise money for a memorial to those who died on the Mier Expedition

August. Camp Colorado moved by Major Earl Van Dorn to Coleman County

August 4. Llano County, named for the plains, created and organized

August 5. Milam Male and Female Institute chartered at Boston in Bowie County

August 7. Waco Female Seminary established at Waco

September 1. Mantua Seminary, supported by the Mantua, Texas, Masonic Lodge, chartered

September 1. Texas and New Orleans Railroad chartered

September 1. Houston Tap and Brazoria Railway Company chartered

September 1. Sabine and Galveston Bay Railroad and Lumber Company chartered

October. Texas Monumental and Military Institute opened near La Grange

1857

Clay County, named for Henry Clay, created

Montague County, named for Daniel Montague, created

Palo Pinto County organized

Colorado College, first Lutheran College in Texas, founded at Columbus, Texas

Waco Female Academy established at Waco by the Methodist Church

Texas School for the Deaf (then called the Asylum for the Deaf) opened at Austin

Jack County organized

The Guagejohe, a Comanche tribe, reported living on the Llano Estacado

Camp San Felipe established at site of present Del Rio as an outpost of Fort Clark

Fort Hudson, originally called the Camp on the San Pedro, established in Val Verde County

San Antonio's first social club and theater, the Casino Club, chartered with an all-German-Texan membership

The Cart War, attacks by Texan cart drivers on Mexican drivers on the public road between Indianola and San Antonio, began

Red River Station was a major cattle crossing of the Red River for the Chisholm Trail

Daily Times began publication at Jefferson

January. The first edition of the *Texas Almanac* published by the Galveston *News*

May 20. Camp Wood in Real County established

June. A second *Texas Sentinel,* no way related to the first one, began publication at Austin

June 7. Camp Hudson in Val Verde County established to protect the road from San Antonio to El Paso from hostile Indians

June 16. Twenty-five camels brought to Texas were taken to California

June 22. San Antonio-San Diego Mail Route, said to be the first transcontinental mail and passenger line, planned

July. Camp Colorado moved to Jim Ned Creek because of sickness among the soldiers at Mukewater Creek

July 9. The first mail left San Antonio to be delivered on the San Antonio-San Diego Mail Route

November 14. Governor Elisha M. Pease asked the legislature for an emergency company of Texas Rangers to put down the Cart War

December 8. Bee County, named for Barnard E. Bee, created

1858

The following counties were created: Archer, named for Branch T. Archer; Baylor, named for Henry W. Baylor; Chambers, named for Thomas Jefferson Chambers; Coleman, named for R.M. Coleman; Concho, named for the Concho River; Dimmit, named for Philip Dimmit; Duval, named for John C. and Thomas H. Duval; Eastland, named for William M. Eastland; Edwards, named for Haden Edwards; Frio, named for the Frio River; Hardeman, named for Bailey and Thomas Jones Hardeman; Haskell, named for Charles Haskell; Jones, named for Anson Jones, but it later had to be recreated; Kimble, named for George C. Kimble; La Salle, named for Réne Robert Cavelier, Sieur de la Salle; McMullen, named for John McMullen; Menard, named for Michael W. Menard; Runnels, named for Hiram G. Runnels; Throckmorton, named for Dr. William E. Throckmorton; Wilbarger, named for Josiah and Mathias Wilbarger

Present Stephens County created as Buchanan County in honor of President James Buchanan

The German-English School established in San Antonio by the Casino Club

The German Free School Association chartered in Austin

Marianne Wharton College organized at Austin

Rio Grande Female Seminary opened at Brownsville

Sabine Baptist College opened at Milam

The *Whiteman,* a newspaper opposed to Indians, began publication at Jacksboro

Camp Radziminiki, established in Indian Territory as an outpost of Fort Belknap in Young County

Blanco County organized

Natchitoch Indians moved out of Texas into Indian Territory (present Oklahoma)

San Antonio Arsenal founded to provide support to frontier settlements

Risher and Hall Stage Lines was operating mail lines in Texas

The Galveston, Houston, and Henderson Railroad Company constructed the first railroad bridge from the mainland to Galveston

January. Hamilton County, named for General James Hamilton, created

January 19. Bastrop Military Institute, under Methodist Episcopal Church, incorporated

January 21. Indianola Railroad chartered

January 22. Mason County, named for Fort Mason, created·

January 22. Zapata County, named for Colonel Antonio Zapata, created

January 25. Bee County organized

January 26. Millville Male and Female Academy incorporated at Millville in Rusk County

February. Victoria Male Academy was in operation at Victoria

February. Knox County, named for Henry Knox, created, but it remained unsettled

February 1. Original Dawson County created but later abolished

February 1. The following counties were created: Shackelford, named for Dr. John Shackelford; Taylor, named for the Taylor family in the Robertson colony; Wichita, named for the Wichita River; Zavala, named for Lorenzo de Zavala

February 5. New Braunfels Academy chartered

February 7. Mount Enterprise Male and Female Academy chartered in Rusk County

February 13. Freestone County School Association incorporated to found Fairfield Female Academy

February 16. Bosque Female Seminary and Male College chartered

March 29. Major R.S. Neighbors recommended that the Brazos Indian Reservation be abandoned

April 26. Zapata County organized

May. Brown County organized

August 2. Mason County organized

August 8. Hardin County, named for Augustine Blackburn, Benjamin W., Milton A., Franklin, and William Hardin, created

September 15. Butterfield Overland Mail Route (also known as Southern Overland Mail) began operation

September 28. Fort Quitman, named for General John Antony Quitman, established in Hudspeth County

October 2. Neuthard School opened at Round Top

December 26. Battle between Indians under Choctaw Tom and white settlers at Galconda (present Palo Pinto)

1859

Glenblythe Plantation opened in Washington County by Thomas Affleck

The Waggoner Ranch was in operation in Wise County

The building constructed that eventually became the Argyle Hotel in San Antonio

First recorded State Fair of Texas held in Dallas

Anna Judson Female Institute opened at Starrville under Baptist jurisdiction

Fairfield Female Academy opened

Hale Institute opened at Rusk

January 9. Governor Hardin R. Runnels issued proclamation warning all Texas to avoid hostilities against Indians

February 1. The Menger Hotel, one of the most famous hotels in Texas, opened in San Antonio

March 23. Fort Stockton, named for Commodore Robert Field Stockton, opened in present Pecos County

April 30. Camp Van Camp established in Young County

June 11. Orders were issued for complete removal of Indians from the Brazos Indian Reservation

July 13. The Cortina War, named for Juan Nepomuceno Cortina, began in Brownsville

July 31. Brazos Indian Reservation abandoned

August 8. Camp Nowlin established on Little Wichita River as post for men escorting Indians from Brazos Indian Reservation to Indian Territory

August 28. Camp Van Camp abandoned

October 2. Camp Ives in Kerr County established by Lieutenant Wesley Owens

October 8. Salado College had its beginning at a tent meeting at Salado Springs

1860

Marion County, named for General Francis Marion, created and organized

Wilson County, named for James C. Wilson, created and organized

Name of Gilmer Female College changed to Upshur Masonic College

Ladonia Male and Female Institute founded at Ladonia by Baptist Church

San Saba Masonic College established at San Saba

St. Mary's Hall, a girl's school in San Antonio, founded by the Episcopal Church

Texas Baptist College, a school for men, established at Tyler

Disciples of Christ had 2,500 members in Texas

Carpenter's Union founded in Galveston and is now one of the oldest locals in the United States

Blair's Fort established in Eastland County by C.C. Blair

Name of Galveston Wharf and Cotton Press Company changed to Galveston Wharf Company

Thirty percent of all Texans were Negroes

January 7. Houston, Trinity, and Tyler Railroad chartered

January 30. Air Line Railroad Company chartered by William Sledge

February 2. Columbus Tap Railway chartered

February 2. Waco Classical School chartered at Waco

February 6. Fayetteville Male and Female Academy opened at Fayetteville

February 8. Fairfield Female Academy in Freestone County opened

February 8. Salado College chartered

February 8. Texas Medical College chartered to be located near Houston

February 8. Greer County created

February 11. First Clifton Academy in Bosque County established

February 11. Ewing College at La Grange chartered

February 11. Marianne Wharton College chartered under the name, Wharton College

February 11. Waco Female Seminary and Waco Female Academy consolidated and chartered as Waco Female College

February 14. Bright Star Educational Society in Hopkins County chartered

March 13. Camp Ives temporarily abandoned when its troops escorted Robert E. Lee to the Rio Grande

July 29. The press of the *Whiteman* destroyed by fire after which the newspaper relocated at Weatherford

August 18. First issue of the *Alamo Express* published

Fall. Brazos Institute at Galconda (present Palo Pinto) under Brazos River Missionary Baptist Association opened for its first and only term

November 26. Fayette Academy chartered but it was commonly called Fayetteville Academy

December 18. Cynthia Ann Parker recaptured at the battle of the Pease River from Comanches by a company of Texas Rangers

1861

Texas Legislature chose Louis T. Wigfall and Williamson S. Oldham to serve in the Confederate Senate

F.R. Lubbock elected governor over Edward Clark and T.J. Chambers

Peace Party (also called the Loyal League) tried to get support for the Union cause and became known as the Peace Party Conspiracy

Whitfield's Legion organized in Lavaca County to fight in the Civil War

DAVID G. BURNET.

DAVID G. BURNET, the first President of Texas. Engraving
from Homer Thrall, *Pictorial History of Texas* (1879).
— *Photo from The University of Texas
Institute of Texan Cultures.*

Camp Clark founded in Guadalupe County by Governor Edward Clark

Pacaruja Indians reported living in Texas

Clay County temporarily organized but was abandoned because of Civil War

Name of Buchanan County changed to Stephens County to honor Alexander H. Stephens, Vice President of the Confederate States of America

Name of Cass County changed to Davis County to honor Jefferson Davis

January 21. Governor Sam Houston submitted the secession resolutions of South Carolina to the Texas Legislature

January 28. Secession Convention met at Austin

January 28. Camp Ives permanently abandoned

February. A Committee of Public Safety appointed by the first session of the Secession Convention

February 1. Ordinance of Secession passed by the Secession Convention by a vote of 166 to 8

February 7. Texas Legislature passed a law allowing frontier counties to raise companies of minutemen

February 18. Camp Cooper abandoned on orders of General David E. Twiggs

February 23. Referendum in Texas ratified the action of the Secession Convention to take Texas out of the Union

February 26. Camp Colorado abandoned on orders from General David E. Twiggs

March. A group of colonists left Laredo led by Michael James Box to found in Mexico what became known as the Box Colony

March 15. Camp Wood abandoned

March 16. Edward Clark became governor when Sam Houston refused to support the Confederacy

April 18. The *Star of the West* captured by Confederate forces at Matagorda Bay

May. Confederate offensive from Texas invaded Indian Territory (Oklahoma)

May 11. The Austin State Hospital opened under the name of State Lunatic Asylum

July 6. The Texas chapter of the Order of the Sons of Hermann, an organization of German descendants, founded in San Antonio

August-September. Sibley's Brigade formed in San Antonio by Henry Hopkins Sibley

September 2. Waco University opened at Waco under direction of the Baptist Church

September 9. Terry's Texas Rangers mustered at Houston to fight in the Civil War

November. An infantry company known as the Travis Rifles organized in Austin for service in the Confederate army

December. The Frontier Regiment established to provide frontier protection by Texas Rangers

1862

Coleman County tentatively organized but was disrupted by the Civil War

Kendall County, named for George Wilkins Kendall, created

McMullen County organized, but later abandoned because of bandits and lack of population

Camp Groce established near Hempstead to imprison Federal troops in Civil War

Polignac's Brigade, a Texas cavalry unit, ordered into Indian Territory and Arkansas

Waul's Legion organized at Brenham by Thomas W. Waul to serve in the Civil War

California Column organized by Colonel James H. Carleton

Bosqueville Male and Female College founded near Waco by Baptists under the leadership of S.G. O'Bryan

State Fair of Texas formally organized

January. Texas State Military Board created

February. Confederate Texas soldiers defeated federal forces at Valverde, New Mexico

March. Camp Montel in Bandera County established by James M. Norris as a ranger station for the Frontier Regiment

March. Camp Salmon on Eastland-Callahan County line established by James M. Norris as a ranger station for the Frontier Regiment

March. Camp San Saba in McCulloch County established by James M. Norris as a ranger station for the Frontier Regiment

March. Camp Davis established in Gillespie County by James M. Norris as a ranger station for the Frontier Regiment

March 7. John Bell Hood assumed command of the Texas Brigade that later became known as Hood's Texas Brigade

March 17. Camp Cureton established in Archer County as a ranger station for the Frontier Regiment

March 17. Camp Belknap established in Young County by James M. Norris as a ranger station for the Frontier Regiment

March 21. Camp Breckenridge in Stephens County established by James M. Norris as a ranger station for the Frontier Regiment

March 23. Camp Pecan in Callahan County established by James M. Norris as a ranger station for the Frontier Regiment

March 23. Camp Collier in Brown County established by James M. Norris as a ranger station for the Frontier Regiment

March 26. Camp McMillan in San Saba County established by James M. Norris as a ranger station for the Frontier Regiment

March 29. Camp Llano in Mason County established by James M. Norris as a ranger station for the Frontier Regiment

March 31. Camp Verde near old Camp Verde in Kerr County established by James M. Norris as a ranger station for the Frontier Regiment

April. Camp Nueces in Uvalde County established by James M. Norris as a ranger station for the Frontier Regiment

April 4. Camp Dix in Uvalde County established by James M. Norris as a ranger station for the Frontier Regiment

April 7. Camp Rabb in Bexar Territory established by James M. Norris as a ranger station for the Frontier Regiment

May 14. The 8th Texas Infantry Battalion organized in Refugio County by Alfred Marmaduke Hobby

July. First of three conferences held in Marshall by governors of western states of the Confederacy

August 10. Battle of the Nueces occurred near Fort Clark

August 29. Fort Davis recaptured by Union forces after being controlled by Confederates

September. Parsons' Brigade, composed of Texas units, formed in Arkansas for service in the Civil War

October. Walker's Texas Division organized at Camp Nelson, near Austin, Arkansas, to fight in the Civil War and named for Major General John George Walker

October. Ector's Brigade of the Confederate army organized

October. The Great Hanging at Gainesville occurred because of the "Peace Party Conspiracy"

October 4. Battle of Galveston began

November. Ross' Brigade or Ross' Cavalry Brigade, a Confederate army unit composed chiefly of Texans, organized at Grenada, Mississippi

1863

Burr's Ferry on the Sabine River became a critical river crossing during the Civil War

Pendleton Murrah defeated T. J. Chambers for governor

Fort Esperanza built on Matagorda Island by slave labor as a Confederate post

August 15. Second of three conferences held in Marshall by governors of western states of the Confederacy

August 18. Official reports showed Texas to have four gun factories in operation

September 5. Battle of Sabine Pass fought

October. Confederate arsenal moved from Arkansas to Tyler, Texas

November. Granbury's Texas Brigade formed to fight in the Civil War

November 3. The Rio Grande Campaign began by Union forces to stop trade from Texas to Mexico across the Rio Grande

December 11. San Saba Masonic College chartered

1864

The Guisole Indians reported by Manuel Orozco y Berra as living in Texas

Texas Medical College finally organized as Galveston Medical College at Galveston

January 1. Federal forces had control of the Texas coast from the mouth of the Rio Grande to Matagorda Peninsula

March. The Red River Campaign of the Civil War began

April. Collin County, named for Collin McKinney, organized

April 8. The Battle of Mansfield was the last Union attempt to invade Texas during the Civil War

April 9. Camp Ford near Tyler in Smith County established after the Battle of Mansfield to detain Federal prisoners of war

May 25. Henderson Masonic Female Institute at Henderson incorporated

July 30. Colonel John S. Ford recaptured Brownsville from Federal control

August 9. The Ellison Springs Indian Fight occurred in Eastland County

November 26. First battle of Adobe Walls occurred

1865

Male and female departments of Baylor University separated by the Baptist State Convention and the girls' department became known as Baylor Female College (now Mary Hardin-Baylor College)

Carlton College, established at Kentuckytown, Texas

Concrete College, a Baptist institution in DeWitt County, established

Eastern Texas Female College in Tyler became Charnwood Institute when it was acquired by C.T. Hand

Die Freie Presse fuer Texas, a German language newspaper, began publication in San Antonio

Early-Hasley Feud began in Bell County

Local union of the Typographical Union organized in Houston

The Benevolent and Protective Order of Elks founded nationally and shortly thereafter in Texas

January 8. Battle of Dove Creek occurred near San Angelo

May. The Shelby Expedition, led by Joseph Orville Shelby, moved into Mexico

May 11. Battle of Palmito Ranch occurred near Brownsville

May 15. Third of three conferences held in Marshall by governors of western states of the Confederacy

May 25. Fort Sabine at the entrance to Sabine Pass surrendered to Federal troops

June 11. In the demoralization of the breaking up of the Confederacy the treasury in Austin was robbed of about $1,700

June 19. General Gordon Granger arrived at Galveston and proclaimed United States authority over Texas at the end of the Civil War

June 19. General Gordon Granger declared slaves to be free in Texas, and it became known as ".Juneteenth"

July 17. General Edward R.S. Canby appointed commander of the Department of Louisiana and Texas

July 21. A.J. Hamilton appointed provisional governor of Texas and began the Reconstruction era in Texas

August 15. Kicking Bird signed treaty with the United States government in which Kickapoo Indians accepted the reservation plan

September 1. Camp Liendo near Hempstead used as a campsite by George A. Custer

September 22. The first national bank to be chartered in Texas, the First National Bank of Galveston, was organized

October. San Antonio *Express* began publication

November 15. Andrew Jackson Hamilton, provisional governor of Texas, issued a proclamation for an election of delegates to a new constitutional convention

December. The Freedmen's Bureau began to function in Texas

December 13. *Texas Baptist Herald* first issued in Houston as the official organ of the Baptist Church in Texas

1866

First Congregational Church established in Texas at Corpus Christi

Case School reopened in Victoria after the Civil War

Cleburne Male and Female Institute established by the Baptist Church

Lamar Female Seminary opened in Paris

Present Our Lady of the Lake College had its beginning in San Antonio

Pennington College opened at Pennington in Trinity County

Saloons were required to close on Sundays

Texas Transportation Company chartered

Houston Direct Navigation Company chartered

Western Union Telegraph Company began operations in Texas

First producing oil well dug near Melrose by Lynis T. Barrett

Hood County, named for John Bell Hood, created and organized

Ku Klux Klan founded in Pulaski, Tennessee, and soon spread to Texas

Rio Grande Railroad chartered

Galveston Medical Journal, first medical periodical in Texas, began publication

Goodnight-Loving Trail opened

January 4. Fort Jacksboro established in Jack County

January 8. Election held to elect delegates to a new constitutional convention

February 7. Constitutional Convention convened in Austin

March 6. Resolution introduced in legislature to create a state east of the Trinity River called East Texas

July. Greer County organized

September 11. The Screwmen's Benevolent Association of Galveston, a trade union of longshoremen, established

September 24. Bayland Orphans' Home for Boys chartered

October. The first Sisters of Divine Providence arrived in Texas from Alsace-Lorraine

October 22. Houston and Great Northern Railroad Company chartered

October 25. The Sisters of Charity of the Incarnate Word arrived in Galveston to work in Texas

November 5. Waco and Northwestern Railroad Company chartered as the Waco Tap Railroad, but it was never built under that name

November 12. Texas Legislature passed a law making "mavericking" illegal

December 5. Henderson Masonic Female Institute destroyed by a tornado

1867

Byars' Institute in Chambers County opened by Tyron Baptist Association

Carlton College moved to Bonham

Stonewall Institute established at Big Hill in Gonzales County

The 6666 (Four Sixes) ranch established in Denton County by Samuel Burk Burnett

Chisholm Trail marked by Tim F. Hersey

Lee-Peacock Feud in Fannin, Grayson, Collin, and Hunt counties, began

San Antonio National Cemetery established in San Antonio

Knights of the White Camelia started in New Orleans and soon spread to Texas

Waco Examiner established at Waco

January 15. Bayland Orphans' Home for Boys organized in Houston

February 15. The case of *Texas* v. *White* filed in the United States Supreme Court which raised the question of whether Texas actually seceded from the Union

March. Hopewell Institute established in Navarro County by the Baptist Church

July. The so-called "carpetbag era" began when Governor James W. Throckmorton was removed from office

July 31. Fort Griffin, named for Major General Charles Griffin, established near present Albany

September. McVeigh School, a seminary for girls, opened in Austin

November. Sutton-Taylor Feud began at Mason

November 5. Laureles Ranch established by Captain Mifflin Kenedy

November 26. Fort Richardson, named for Israel B. Richardson, established at Jacksboro

December. Camp Hatch (later Fort Concho), named for Major John P. Hatch, established in Tom Green County

1868

Coronal Institute founded at San Marcos

Brazos Eagle began publication at Bryan

Garrison from Fort Bliss moved to Concordia Ranch and became known as Camp Concordia

Latimer County, named for Albert Hamilton Latimer, created by the constitutional convention of 1868-1869, but it was never organized

Seven-D Ranch established in Pecos County by Peter Gallagher

January. Name of Camp Hatch (later Fort Concho) changed to Camp Kelly in honor of Michael J. Kelly

February. Negroes voted for the first time in Texas

March. Name of Camp Kelly changed to Fort Concho for the near-by river

May 30. Denton *Monitor* began publication

June 1. Constitutional Convention of 1868 assembled in Austin

September. Name of Bastrop Military Institute changed to Texas Military Institute

1869

Charnwood Institute in Tyler became coeducational

Courtney Male and Female School in Grimes County opened

Dallas Male and Female College established by local Baptists

Mount Calvary Seminary chartered in Dallas County

Rusk Educational Association organized at Rusk

Richland County created by the Constitutional Convention of 1868-1869, but it was never legalized or organized

San Jacinto County, named for the battle of San Jacinto, created

Webster County created by the Constitutional Convention, but it was never organized or legalized by the legislature

Medical Association of Texas reorganized as Texas State Medical Association

Edmund J. Davis elected governor of Texas

Sutton-Taylor Feud continued

The Loyal Union League was most effective in the election of 1869 in keeping blacks active as voters and loyal to the Republican Party

The Ledger began publication at Fairfield

April 15. United States Supreme Court, in *Texas* v. *White*, ruled that the union was insoluable

June 24. Buffalo Bayou Ship Channel organized to build a channel to Houston

July. Constitution of 1869 approved by the voters of Texas

July. Early-Hasley Feud ended with the killing of Jim McRae

September 23. Trinity University opened at Tehuacana under Presbyterian sponsorship

1870

Corsicana Female Literary Institute sold to Corsicana Masonic Lodge

First Evangelical Lutheran College established at Rutersville

Mount Calvary Seminary came under Baptist supervision and name changed to Dallas Male and Female College

Pennington College chartered

Sherman Institute established at Sherman

Delta County, named for the local geographical features, created and organized

San Jacinto County recreated and organized

First sizeable group of Chinese moved to Texas to help build a railroad

Census showed 364 Swedes in Texas

The first of the Holy Cross Sisters came to Texas to establish schools

Second Camp Montel established in Uvalde County

An estimated 1,500 miles of telegraph wire existed in Texas

United Friends of Temperance and its juvenile society, Bands of Hope, organized in Texas

The Rump Senate of the Twelfth Texas Legislature took control

A Negro Longshoremen's Association chartered

Waco Tap Railroad purchased and rechartered as the Waco and Northwestern Railroad Company

Manufacturing of cooling devices began in Texas cities

February 25. Howard Bill introduced in Congress to create three states in Texas

May 5. Ku Klux Klan reported to be active in the Nacogdoches area

June 9. Rains County, named for Emory Rains, created

June 10. Texas Military Institute (formerly Bastrop Military Institute) moved from Bastrop to Austin

July. State Police organized as a part of Reconstruction

July. Southern Transcontinental Railroad Company chartered

July 27. Galveston, Harrisburg, and San Antonio Railway Company chartered

August 5. International Railroad Company chartered

December. Lieutenant H. B. Mellon of the 6th Cavalry stationed at Camp Wichita

December 7. The Salt War began for control of the salt deposits near El Paso

1871

Aransas County, named for Rio Nuestra Señora de Aranzazu, created and organized

Name of Davis County changed to Cass County, its original name

Frio County organized

Pecos County, named for the Pecos River, created

Maverick and Menard counties organized

Governor E. J. Davis proposed the division of Texas into four states

Masonic Lodge of Rusk bought Rusk Educational Association and opened Rusk Masonic Institute

Name of Sherman Institute changed to North Texas Female College

East Line and Red River Railroad Company established

Tyler Tap Railroad chartered

Office of inspector of hides and animals created

March 3. Texas Pacific Railroad Company chartered by the United States Congress

March 25. Regimental headquarters of Fourth United States

MIRABEAU BUONOPARTE Lamar, elected President of
Texas on November 10, 1838. Portrait by C.B. Normann.
— *Photo from Texas State Library.*
Copy from The University of Texas Institute of Texan Cultures.

Cavalry moved to Fort Richardson at Jacksboro

April 5. Henderson Male and Female College at Henderson chartered

April 17. The Agricultural and Mechanical College of Texas (Texas A & M University) created by the Texas Legislature

May. Lamar Female Seminary chartered

May 17. The Salt Creek Massacre occurred near Graham in Young County

July 26. The first issue of the Austin *Statesman* appeared

August. A boundary dispute known as the Brownsville Wharf case began

August 3. Galveston Historical Society, the first such organization in Texas, organized

August 5. A group of Texas taxpayers met in Austin to protest the extravagance of the administration of Governor E. J. Davis and it became known as the Taxpayers' Convention of 1871

November 1. Charter of Hermann's University repealed

December. First organization of teachers in Texas formed at Austin

December 2. Dallas and Wichita Railway Company chartered

1872

Clark Seminary, a girls' school in Houston, opened

Davilla Institute founded in Milam County by local Baptists

Paul Quinn College established at Waco by the African Methodist Episcopal Church

The *Ledger* moved from Fairfield to Mexia

The *Texas New Yorker,* a monthly magazine to promote Texas, published in New York City by George H. Sweet

The Hashknife brand of the Hashknife Ranch used in Taylor County

Point Bolivar Lighthouse constructed as a guide to ships

Nakanawan Indians reported in Texas

The Georgia Army, a vigilante-type organization, organized in Montague County

March 22. The first lodge of the Knights of Pythias established in Texas at Houston

May 2. Name of Texas Pacific Railroad Company changed to Texas and Pacific

May 13. The Giddings-Clark Election Contest, a Reconstruction era conflict, came to an end when D. C. Giddings instead of William T. Clark took the seat in Congress

June. The first major labor strike in Texas occurred against the Houston and Texas Central Railway

1873

Alexander Institute established at Kilgore

Galveston Medical College reorganized under the name of the Texas Medical College and Hospital

Granbury College, essentially a high school, established in Hood County by the Methodist Episcopal Church, South

Jacksonville Collegiate Institute opened at Jacksonville

Wiley College, oldest Negro college west of the Mississippi River, established at Marshall by the Methodist Episcopal Church

The Sisters of St. Mary of Namur, a Belgian order, arrived in Waco to establish schools

Fort Worth and Denver City Railway Company chartered

Huntsville Branch Railway Company merged with the International-Great Northern

International and Great Northern Railroad chartered

Athens *Bulletin* began publication in Henderson County

Texas Cumberland Presbyterian began publication at Tehuacana

Ammonia compression refrigeration born at Jefferson, Texas, by David Boyle

Horrell-Higgins Feud in Lampasas County began

Rockwall County, named for a subterranean "rock wall," created and organized

Waller County, named for Edwin Waller, created and organized

January. A second organization known as the Travis Rifles formed at Austin

April 22. After the Democrats regained control of the legislature, the law creating the State Police was repealed

May 8. Marvin College chartered by the Northwest Texas Methodist Conference at Waxahachie

May 8. Rusk Masonic Institute chartered

May 13-15. First convention of the Texas Veterans Association held at Houston

May 17. Hallville Masonic Institute chartered in Harrison County

May 27. Clay County reorganized

May 28. Gulf, Colorado, and Santa Fe Railway Company chartered

June 2. Wegefarth County, named for C. Wegefarth, created in the disputed area of Greer County

June 21. Name of Dallas *Herald* changed to Dallas *Weekly Herald*

June 28. Gregg County, named for General John Gregg, created and organized

July. First Grange (Patrons of Husbandry) founded in Texas at Salado by R. A. Baird

August 5. Packsaddle Mountain Fight occurred in Llano County
September. Add-Ran College established at Thorp Spring
October 6. Southwestern University opened for its first session at Georgetown
December 2. Eastland County organized

1874

St. Mary's Academy established at Austin by the Sisters of the Holy Cross

Indians were raiding near Camp Charlotte in Irion County, but the soldiers were powerless to stop them

Camp County named for John Lafayette Camp organized

Lee County, named for Robert E. Lee, created

Four Sixes Ranch (6666) moved to the vicinity of Wichita Falls

T Bar Ranch began in San Saba County by Margaret Fleming

Dallas *Daily Herald* began publication

Frontier Battalion, composed of Texas Rangers, created to protect the Texas frontier

Galveston Public Library chartered as the first municipal library in Texas

March 13. Tom Green County, named for General Thomas Green, created

April 29. The Henderson and Overton Branch Railroad Company chartered

May. Name of Paine Female Institute changed to Paine Male and Female Institute

May 4. Rusk Transportation Company organized in Rusk to provide whatever form of transportation necessary to connect Rusk with the outside world

Summer and Fall. The Red River Indian War was directed against Indians leaving the reservations in present Oklahoma

June 27. Second battle of Adobe Walls occurred

September 12. Shackelford County organized

September 12. Buffalo Wallow Fight occurred in Wheeler County

October. Camp Kenny in Stephens County opened as a patrolling post of the Frontier Regiment

December. Blanco Masonic University was projected

1875

Keatchie College moved from Keatchie, Louisiana, to Nacogdoches, Texas, and used the buildings of Nacogdoches University

Riverside Institute established by J. R. Malone near Dallas

Sabine Valley University at Hemphill had its beginning with the Mt. Zion Baptist Association

73

Texas Female Institute established in Austin under Baptist sponsorship

Sheep wars occurred on the Goodnight Ranch range on the Texas-New Mexico line

Bill to protect buffalo from extermination defeated in the legislature because of influence of General Philip H. Sheridan

The Farmer's Alliance organized originally in Texas

Peña Station established near Hebbronville in Jim Wells County

Rose growing industry in Texas began in Tyler

Pecos and Presidio counties organized

Somervell County, named for Alexander Somervell, created and organized

January 6. The first of the Sisters of Mercy arrived at Indianola from New Orleans

January 18. The third railroad with the name, Texas Western Railroad, created under the name of Texas Western Narrow Gauge Railroad

February. Building was planned and land was sought for Blanco Masonic University

February 6. Known first as Texas University, Southwestern University chartered by the Methodist Church at Georgetown

February 10. Crockett County, named for David Crockett, created

February 18. Mason County War (really a feud), also known as the "Hoodoo War," began

March 11. Houston, East and West Texas Railway chartered

March 13. Morris County, named for W. W. Morris, created

March 18. Corpus Christi, San Diego, and Rio Grande Narrow Gauge Railroad chartered

April 30. Franklin County, named for Judge Benjamin C. Franklin, organized

June 5. Fort Elliott established in Wheeler County and named for Major Joel H. Elliott

June 14. Jefferson Davis offered the presidency of the newly-established Agricultural and Mechanical College of Texas (Texas A & M University)

June 26. Methodist Episcopal Church, South purchased Coronal Institute in San Marcos

June 30. The *Frontier Echo* first published in Jacksboro

September. Stuart Seminary at Austin opened for classes

September 6. Constitutional Convention of 1875 met for the first time in Austin

September 15. First of two great storms struck Indianola and virtually destroyed the town

74

Dallas and Cleburne Railroad chartered

Galveston, Brazos, and Colorado Railroad built

Waxahachie Tap Railroad Company chartered

Centennial Masonic Institute founded in Centennial (later Canaan) in Grayson County

Fredericksburg College founded by German Methodist Church

Sabine Valley University opened at Hemphill

Savoy Male and Female College founded at Savoy in Fannin County

Shilow Baptist Institute established at Whitesboro

South East Texas Male and Female College chartered

Stonewall Seminary, named for Thomas J. "Stonewall" Jackson, established at Woodland in Red River county

Dallas *Evening Times* founded

Street's Weekly (later *Holland's Magazine)* began publication

Department of Insurance, Statistics, and History created

Jones and Plummer Trail to Dodge City, Kansas, opened

The Rath Trail, a road for the buffalo hide business, opened by Charles Rath

Hereford cattle first introduced into Texas by J.F. Brady of Houston

Charles Goodnight drove the first Shorthorn cattle to the Panhandle where he established the JA Ranch

Greenback Movement got its start in Texas

The following counties were created: Armstrong, named for a pioneer family; Bailey, named for Peter J. Bailey; Borden, named for Gail Borden, Jr.; Briscoe, named for Andrew Briscoe; Carson, named for Samuel P. Carson; Castro, named for Henri Castro; Childress, named for George C. Childress; Cochran, named for Robert Cochran; Collingsworth, named for James Collinsworth with a variation in spelling; Cottle, named for George W. Cottle; Dallam, named for James W. Dallam; Deaf Smith, named for Erastus (Deaf) Smith; Dickens, named for the Alamo victim J. Dickens; Fisher, named for Samuel Rhoads Fisher; Gaines, named for James Gaines; Garza, named for a pioneer family; Gray, named for Peter W. Gray; Hale, named for Lieutenant John C. Hale; Hall, named for Warren D.C. Hall; Hansford, named for John M. Hansford; Hardeman, recreated after remaining unsettled since 1858; Hartley, named for Rufus K. and Oliver C. Hartley; Haskell, recreated after remaining unsettled since 1858; Hockley, named for George W. Hockley; Howard, named for Volney Erskine Howard; Hutchinson, named for Anderson Hutchinson; Jones, recreated after remaining unsettled since 1858; Kent, named for Andrew Kent; King, named for William P.King; Knox, recreated after remaining unsettled since 1858; Lipscomb, named for Abner S. Lipscomb; Lubbock, named for Thomas S. Lubbock; Lynn, named for W. Lynn or Linn; Martin, named for Wylie Martin; Mitchell, named for Eli Mitchell; Moore, named for Commodore E. W. Moore; Motley, named for Dr. Junius William Mottley; Nolan, named for Philip Nolan; Ochiltree, named for William Beck Ochiltree; Oldham, named for Williamson Simpson Oldham; Parmer, named for Martin Parmer; Potter, named for Robert Potter; Randall, named for Horace Randal; Roberts, named for John S. and Oran M. Roberts; Scurry, named for William R. Scurry; Sherman, named for Sidney Sherman; Stonewall, named for Thomas J. "Stonewall" Jackson; Terry, named for Benjamin Franklin Terry; Yoakum, named for Henderson Yoakum

The following counties were organized: Coleman, Duval, Kimble, McCulloch, Stephens

February. A new *Texas Presbyterian* began publication

February 15. Constitution of 1876 approved by the voters of Texas

August 4. Franco-Texan Land Company chartered and eventually owned approximately 600,000 acres

August 21. The following counties were created: Andrews, named for Richard Andrews; Dawson, named for Nicholas M. Dawson; Floyd, named for Delphin Ward Floyd; Lamb, named for George A. Lamb; Swisher, named for John G. Swisher; Wheeler, named for Royal T. Wheeler

August 21. Wegefarth County abolished when other Panhandle counties were created

October 4. Texas A & M opened for classes for the first time

December 15. Black Horse, a Comanche chief also called Nigger Horse, led his braves off the Fort Sill Reservation to raid in Texas

1877

Name of Keatchie College in Nacogdoches changed back to Nacogdoches University

Mary Nash College established at Sherman as Sherman Female Institute

Paluxy College opened near Glen Rose in Somervell County

Tillotson College, a college for blacks, chartered at Austin by the Congregational Churches

North Texas Educational Association organized at Dallas

T Anchor Ranch began when Leigh Dyer drove a herd of cattle to Palo Duro Creek

The LIT Ranch owned by George W. Littlefield started on the Canadian River

The LX Ranch established on Ranch Creek, a tributary of the

Canadian River, by W.H. Bates and David T. Beals

Callahan County, named for James Hughes Callahan, organized

McMullen County reorganized

Central and Montgomery Railway chartered to run in timber belt of East Texas

February 15. The Northwest Texas Cattle Raisers' Association founded at Graham

May. The first division of the Nolan or "Lost Nigger" Expedition started in pursuit of marauding Indians

July. The second unit of the Nolan or "Lost Nigger" Expedition started in pursuit of marauding Indians

July 27. Denison and Southeastern Railway Company chartered

1878

Austin College moved from Huntsville to Sherman

Dallas College opened under Baptist ownership

Jacksonville Institute opened in the buildings of the old Jacksonville Collegiate Institute

Montgomery Institute opened in Seguin under Episcopal sponsorship

Whitesboro Normal School established at Whitesboro

Matador Ranch started by A.M. Britton and H.H. Campbell

Longview and Sabine Valley Railway stopped construction after failing to attract investors

The *Texas Christian* began publication at Thorp Spring by the Disciples of Christ

Military forces occupied Camp Grierson in Reagan County

Oran M. Roberts elected governor

Nacogdoches Archives transferred from the secretary of state's office to the State Archives

Taylor County organized

March 12. First convention of the Texas Greenback Party met in Austin

March 18. First telephone line established in Galveston by A.H. Belo

April 24. Denison and Pacific Railway chartered

May 16. Georgetown Railroad Company chartered

August 10. Dallas, Palestine, and Southeast Railroad chartered

September 2. South East Texas Male and Female College opened at Jasper

1879

Texas legislature provided for the establishment of Prairie View State Normal School

Texas legislature incorporated the Sisters of Divine Providence

77

so that Our Lady of the Lake College could be founded

Austin Teachers Association organized

Chicago, Texas, and Mexican Central Railway chartered

Texas Central Railway Company chartered

Texas and St. Louis Railway chartered

Quaker Colony founded by Paris Cox in Crosby County

Barbed wire first offered for sale in Texas by H.B. Sanborn

Cuban cigar leaf tobacco grown successfully on a commercial scale near Willis in Montgomery County

The Cotton Jammer's Association, a black longshoremen's group, formed as a labor union

Rountree Stage Stand was the only stage stop on the San Patricio Trail between Fairview and Oakville

The Farmers' Alliance reorganized in Parker County

The earliest publication of what eventually became the Fort Worth *Star-Telegram*

Natural gas industry began in Texas in Washington County

Approximately 104,000 acres of wheat were harvested

Throckmorton and Wheeler counties organized

January 4. *Frontier Echo* moved from Jacksboro and began publication as the Fort Griffin *Echo*

February 6. The *Texan*, the first Czech language newspaper in Texas, began publication at La Grange

March 11. Concho County organized

March 31. Louisiana Western Extension Railroad chartered

July. Name of the *Texan*, the Czech language newspaper, changed to *Slovan*

July 14. Legislature passed Fifty Cent Act to sell public land at fifty cents per acre to pay the public debt and establish a permanent school fund

August. The first newspaper in the Texas Panhandle, the Clarendon *News*, established by Lewis Henry Carhart

August 21. First telephone exchange opened in Galveston

October 10. Sam Houston Normal Institute opened at Huntsville

December 2. Buckner Orphans Home opened in Dallas

December 22. Fort Sam Houston named for Sam Houston, occupied

1880

Calhoun College at Kingston opened

Lagarto College opened at Lagarto

Laredo Seminary (later known as Holding Institute) founded at Laredo by the Methodist Episcopal Church, South

Rock Hill Institute opened near Minden in Rusk County

The Academy of Science of Texas organized

Christian Messenger, journal of the Disciples of Christ, published in Bonham and later in Dallas

Christian Preacher, weekly periodical of the Churches of Christ, published at McKinney

Morris Ranch established in Gillespie and Kerr Counties by Francis Morris

U Lazy S Ranch located in Crosby County by John B. and C.C. Slaughter

The OX Ranch established in Childress County by A. and J. Forsyth

The Llano Cattle Company, operator of the Curry-Comb Ranch near Post, Texas, organized

First pure-bred Jersey cattle brought to Texas

Fort Peña Colorado established in Brewster County

First officially recorded labor strike by draymen

Dimmit, La Salle, Oldham, and Runnels counties organized

January 22. Savoy Male and Female College chartered

February 18. Kansas and Gulf Short Line Railroad Company chartered

February 19. Houston *Post* established by Gail Borden Johnson

March 6. Missouri, Kansas, and Texas Extension Railway Company chartered to take over the Denison and Southeastern Railway

March 23. Denison and Pacific Railway taken over by Missouri, Kansas, and Texas Extension Railway Company

April 29. East Texas Railroad Company chartered

May 19. Texas Press Association organized at Houston

June 29. Austin Teachers Association and North Texas Educational Association met at Mexia and formed the Texas State Teachers Association

July 27. Archer County organized

August. *Texas Journal of Education* established at Austin

September 27. Buckner Orphans Home moved to permanent quarters on the outskirts of Dallas

November 17. New York, Texas, and Mexican Railway, also known as "Macaroni Road," chartered

1881

Bishop College established at Marshall

Dripping Springs Academy established by local residents but later taken over by Baptists

McMullen College opened under Baptist sponsorship at Tilden in McMullen County

Parker Institute established at Whitt in Parker County

CAPITOL HOTEL, originally designed by Thomas William Ward for use as the National Capitol in Houston.

— Photo from Barker Texas History Center, Austin, Texas. Copy from The University of Texas Institute of Texan Cultures.

Paul Quinn College chartered by the state and moved to Waco

Name of East Line and Red River Railroad Company changed to Sherman, Shreveport, and Southern Railroad

Name of Texas and St. Louis Railway changed to the Texas and St. Louis Company of Texas

Name of the Waxahachie Tap Railroad Company changed to Central Texas and Northwestern Railroad Company when it was bought by the Houston and Texas Central Railroad Company

Southwestern Telegraph and Telephone Company organized

The Cowden Ranch began in the South Plains

The Frying Pan Ranch began in Potter and Randall counties

The Hashknife brand sold to Continental Land and Cattle Company of St. Louis, Missouri

Pitchfork brand of the Pitchfork Ranch bought by D.B. Gardner and J.S. Godwin

Texas Siftings, a humor magazine, began publication at Austin

Mitchell, Jones, and Wilbarger counties organized

January 10. Nolan County organized

January 17. Tillotson College opened at Austin

January 20. San Antonio *Light* began publication

March 9. Law passed providing for sheep inspectors and the quarantine of diseased sheep

March 15. City of Abilene established by Texas and Pacific Railroad and West Texas cattlemen

April 12. Gonzales Branch Railroad Company chartered

April 29. Austin and Northwestern Railroad Company chartered

June 1. Telephone exchange opened in Dallas

June 6. Fort Worth University chartered as Texas Wesleyan College by the Northern Methodist Church

June 14. Laredo *Times* began publication

June 17. Abilene *Reporter-News* begun as a weekly paper called the *Reporter*

June 30. Name of the Corpus Christi, San Diego, and Rio Grande Narrow Gauge Railroad changed to Texas-Mexican Railway Company

July. Incarnate Word College chartered in San Antonio by the Sisters of Charity of Incarnate Word, a Catholic order

July 28. Paris and Great Northern Railroad Company incorporated and was beginning of the Frisco system

September 6. Main campus of the University of Texas located in Austin and Galveston chosen for the Medical Branch

September 7. Fort Worth University opened under the name Texas Wesleyan College

September 28. Trinity and Sabine Railway Company chartered

November. Capitol of Texas burned

1882

Convent of the Sacred Heart, a teacher-training school for the Sisters of Saint Dominic, established at Houston

Wiley College at Marshall chartered

Marshall and Northwestern Railroad established

Rio Grande and Pecos Railroad founded

The *Mesquiter* began publication at Mesquite

Matador Land and Cattle Company, Limited organized to purchase the Matador Ranch

Square and Compass Ranch started by the Nave-McCord Cattle Company

Fort Hancock, named for General Winfield Scott Hancock, established in Hudspeth County

Howard County organized

Women's Christian Temperance Union introduced in Texas

Texas Legislature appropriated three million dollars to finance construction of new capitol

Donley County, named for Stockton P. Donley, created

January 10. Two-thirds of Dallam County became the property of the Capitol Freehold Land and Investment Company, Limited

March. Sweetwater *Advance* began publication at Sweetwater

Summer. Wichita County organized

July 15. Texas Bar Association temporarily organized at Galveston

September 29. The first of the Dominican Sisters arrived in Galveston from Somerset, Ohio

December 12. Texas Bar Association permanently organized at Galveston

December 18. Galveston, Sabine and St. Louis Railway Company chartered

1883

Blanco Masonic University stock transferred to Blanco Masonic High School

Blinn Memorial College, originally Mission Institute, founded at Brenham by Southern German Conference of the Methodist Episcopal Church

Buffalo Gap College in Taylor County opened by Cumberland Presbyterian Church

Tyler Female College established at Tyler by the Presbyterian Church

The Texas Collection of the University of Texas began

The Pitchfork Land and Cattle Company organized to operate the Pitchfork Ranch

The "Rocking Chair Ranche Company, Limited" established in Collingsworth and Wheeler counties

Two Circles Bar established by O.J. Wiren

Texas School Journal established

The Potter and Blocker, or Potter and Bacon, Cattle Trail laid out

Hereford cattle introduced into Texas Panhandle by Charles Goodnight

Reeves County, named for George R. Reeves, created

Edwards County organized

Terrell State Hospital established in Terrell

First long distance telephone line built between Galveston and Houston

January 6. Fort Griffin *Echo* moved to Albany and became the Albany *Echo*

January 6. The first *Texas Law Review,* a weekly newspaper, began publication at Austin

January 22. Fifty Cent Act repealed

March 24. Cowboy Strike in the Panhandle started

April. Law passed to require sheep to be free of scab before they could be moved across a county line

April 12. The state Land Board created by the legislature

April 14. The Land Fraud Board created by the legislature

April 23. The Alamo church property was purchased from the Roman Catholic Church by the state of Texas and placed in the custody of the city of San Antonio

July 19. Erie Telegraph and Telephone Company established at Austin

September 15. The University of Texas formally opened at Austin

1884

Austin School of Theology of the Presbyterian Church was opened

College Hill Institute opened in Parker County

Guadalupe Colored College in Seguin established by Baptists

Parker Institute at Whitt taken over by the Whitt Methodist Church and chartered by the state

Springtown Male and Female Institute founded at Springtown in Parker County

Weatherford Masonic Institute of Weatherford renamed Cleveland College

Del Rio *Dot,* the first newspaper in the city, established

Fannin Farmers' Review began publication as a Populist newspaper in Bonham

Firm Foundation, a newspaper of the Church of Christ, established at Austin

Dallas Terminal Railway and Union Depot Company chartered

Galveston and Western Railroad built

San Antonio and Aransas Pass Railway begun

San Juan Plantation started in Hidalgo County

The LS Ranch owned by W.M.D. Lee and Lucien Scott established in Oldham County

Two-Buckle Ranch started in Crosby County by the Kentucky Cattle Company

The Western Land and Livestock Company organized in Davenport, Iowa, to buy land in Texas

First recorded coal production reported in Texas

The Lily-White Movement of the Republican Party came into the open

Office of state superintendent of public instruction established by the legislature

Hardeman, Martin, and Scurry counties organized

January 8. Legislative special session opened that passed a law that made fence cutting a felony

February 25. Zavala County organized

March 24. Day Land and Cattle Company organized in Austin

September. Blanco Masonic High School merged with Blanco public schools

October 14. The Belknap Rifles, a San Antonio military company, organized

November. Kyle Seminary chartered at San Marcos

November 12. Treaty of 1884 signed between the United States and Mexico to settle a boundary dispute

1885

Bishop College chartered

The name, Buffalo Gap College, adopted for the college at Buffalo Gap

Grayson College founded at Whitewright

St. Edward's College, a Catholic institution, chartered

Saint Ignatius Academy (later Our Lady of Victory College) founded in Fort Worth

William Carey Crane College established at Independence

Terrell State Hospital opened

Athens *Review* began publication in Henderson County

T.E. Boren was publisher of the *Panola Watchman* in Carthage

Svoboda, a Czech language newspaper, established at La Grange

Capitol Freehold Land and Investment Company, Limited incorporated in London to raise money to stock the XIT Ranch

The Cedar Valley Lands and Cattle Company, an English company, purchased the T Anchor Ranch in Randall County

The **IOA** Ranch in Lubbock County established by Western Land and Livestock Company

XIT Ranch established in the Texas Panhandle

Name of Marshall and Northwestern Railroad changed to the Paris, Marshall, and Sabine Pass Railroad

The Texarkana and Northern Railway Company succeeded by Texarkana and Fort Smith Railway Company

The Crazy Well, with curative water, discovered at Mineral Wells

First creamery in Texas established at Terrell

First reported Japanese in Texas lived in Dallas County

Haskell County organized

March. Midland County, so-named because of its location halfway between Fort Worth and El Paso, created and organized

April 5. The *Morning Chronicle* and the *Evening Journal* combined to create the present Houston *Post*

May 2. Val Verde County, named for the battle of Val Verde (Spanish for green valley), organized after being created earlier in the year

May 25. San Saba Masonic College rechartered under Methodist sponsorship as San Saba College

June 13. Fort Worth and New Orleans Railway Company chartered

July. Texas Bankers Association organized at Lampasas

July 27. St. Edward's University chartered as a Catholic institution at Austin

Fall. Prairie View State Normal School opened for its first term

September. Willis Male and Female College opened at Willis

October 1. Dallas *Morning News* began publication as a north Texas branch of the Galveston *News*

1886

Baylor University and Waco University were consolidated

Baylor Female College (now Mary Hardin-Baylor College) moved to Belton where it was popularly known as Baylor Belton

Belton Academy established

Central College chartered in Sulphur Springs under the Methodist Episcopal Church

Liberty Normal and Business College established at Liberty Hill in Williamson County

Mary Allen Junior College (originally Mary Allen Seminary) founded at Crockett

Woman's Missionary Auxiliary to the Texas Baptist Convention organized

Baptist General Association of Texas and the State Convention were combined to form the Baptist General Convention

Dallas Evening *Herald* established

The *Southern Mercury* established as the official publication of the Farmers' Alliance

Bastrop and Taylor Railway Company began construction

Dallas and Greenville Railway Company created

Dallas and Waco Railway Company incorporated

The bankrupt Texas and St. Louis Company of Texas rechartered as the St. Louis, Arkansas, and Texas Railroad

Southwest Railroad Strike affected many Texas railroad workers who were members of the Knights of Labor

First flask (76 pounds) of mercury produced in Texas near Alpine

Dallas Fair and Exposition formally chartered to operate the State Fair of Texas

First effort to organize a People's Party on a statewide basis failed

The Prohibition Party became active in Texas

A group of Carrizo and Tejón Indians were living in South Texas

A few Comecrudo Indians reported still living in Texas

Cotoname Indians reported living in Hidalgo County

Tunica Indians reported living near Beaumont

Crosby County, named for Stephen Crosby, organized

Fisher and Knox counties organized

January 8. Denison and Washita Valley Railroad Company incorporated

July 23. Gainesville, Henrietta, and Western Railway Company chartered

August 19. The second storm that almost destroyed the town struck Indianola

September. San Antonio Academy opened in San Antonio by Dr. William Belcher Seeley

October 27. Name of Bastrop and Taylor Railway Company changed to Taylor, Bastrop, and Houston Railway Company

November 2. Southern Kansas Railway Company of Texas completed a line from Oklahoma to Canadian, Texas

1887

Baylor University moved from Independence to Waco

Calhoun College at Kingston chartered to offer the B.A. degree

Carlton College became a girls' school

Grayson College chartered

Metropolitan College founded at Dallas

Seven Points Academy opened at Seven Points in Collin County

The Farmers' Alliance merged with the Farmers' Union and eventually became a part of the national Farmers' Alliance and Co-operative Union of America

Confederate Home for Men established

Balcones Escarpment named by Robert Thomas Hill

Prohibition amendment failed in a bitter election

State Orphans' Home for White Children established by the legislature at Corsicana

Mexia *Democrat* began publication

Texas School Magazine established

Charter of Fort Worth and Rio Grande Railway Company amended to provide for an extension to Kerrville

Panhandle Railway Company chartered

Lipscomb and Potter counties organized

Brewster County, named for Henry P. Brewster, organized

The following counties were created: Crane, named for William Carey Crane; Ector, named for General Mathew Duncan Ector; Glasscock, named for George W. Glasscock; Schleicher, named for Gustav Schleicher; Upton, named for John Cunningham and William Fulton Upton; Ward, named for Thomas William Ward; Winkler, named for Judge C.M. Winkler

January 27. Denison, Bonham, and New Orleans Railway Company chartered

February 26. Loving County, named for Oliver Loving, created

March. Mills County, named for John T. Mills, created

March 15. Foley County created

March 15. Buchel County created out of Presidio County, but later abolished

March 15. Jeff Davis County, named for Jefferson Davis, created

April 11. Childress County organized

July 22. Panhandle *Herald*, oldest continuously published newspaper in the Panhandle of Texas, began publication from a tent at Panhandle, Texas

October 3. Texas, Sabine Valley, and Northwestern Railway Company chartered

October 17. Deaf, Dumb, and Blind Institute for Colored Youth established near Austin

December 15. Texas League of Professional Baseball Clubs organized at Austin

1888

The University of San Antonio chartered under Methodist sponsorship

Baptist Training Union of Texas organized

Texas Agricultural Experiment Station System established as a part of the Agricultural and Mechanical College of Texas (Texas A & M University)

Paris, Choctaw, and Little Rock Railway Company chartered

The Christian Courier, a newspaper of the Disciples of Christ in Texas, first published in Dallas

Dallas *Times Herald* formed by merging Dallas *Evening Times* and Dallas *Evening Herald*

The *Weekly Dispatch* established as the official publication of San Antonio labor organizations

Election of 1888 was the beginning of the Jaybird-Woodpecker War in Fort Bend County

First electric fence in Texas used on the XIT Ranch

Firt oil refinery built in Nacogdoches County by the Lubricating Oil Company

Texas Pacific Coal Company bought the coal mines and named the camp Thurber

First organization of the People's Party completed

Stonewall County organized

First contest rodeo supposedly held at Canadian, Texas

January 29. Charter of Bayland Orphans' Home for Boys changed to admit girls and changed the name to Bayland Orphans' Home Association

May 16. New Texas capitol officially opened to the public

July 7. R.E. and John Stafford killed as a part of the Stafford-Townsend Feud in Colorado County

August 4. Hale County organized

September. The 02 brand registered by E.L. and A.S. Gage

December. *Baptist News* first published at Honey Grove

1889

Cleveland College at Weatherford united with Granbury College and was renamed Weatherford College

Columbia College established in Van Alstyne, Texas

Daniel Baker College established at Brownwood

Glen Rose Collegiate Institute established in Somervell County by the Presbyterian Church

Name of Kyle Seminary changed to Kyle Baptist Seminary

Llano Estacado Institute organized at Plainview

Name of Mission Institute changed to Blinn Memorial College as result of $20,000 gift by Christian Blinn

Name of Prairie View Normal School changed to Prairie View State Normal and Industrial College

Name of William Carey Crane College changed to Binford University

Midland *Gazette* began publication at Midland

Val Verde County Herald established in Del Rio

Houston Belt and Magnolia Park Railway Company (later Houston, Oaklawn, and Magnolia Park Railway Company) chartered

Lancaster Tap Railroad built, but it never received a charter

Jaybird-Woodpecker War in Fort Bend County began

San Antonio State Hospital established as the Southwestern Lunatic Asylum

Swine Breeders' Association of Texas organized

First Christian Science Church organized in Austin

Mashed O Ranch in Lamb and Bailey counties started in Oklahoma by W.E. and Glen Halsell

Coke County, named for Richard Coke, created and organized

Irion County, named for Robert A. Irion, created and organized

Hansford, Ochiltree, and Roberts counties organized

January. Gatesville State.School for Boys opened at Gatesville

March 17. First general irrigation and water law passed by the legislature

June. Name of Texas Wesleyan College changed to Fort Worth University

June 13. Sherman County organized

June 30. Howard Payne College founded by the Baptist Church

July. Randall County organized

July 2. Weatherford, Mineral Wells, and Northwestern Railway Company chartered

July 15. State Orphans' Home opened at Corsicana

September 10. St. Mary's College, an Episcopal institution in Dallas, opened

October 30. Granite Mountain and Marble Falls City Railroad chartered

November 25. The White Man's Union Association formed at Wharton to maintain white supremacy in politics

1890

Carlisle Military Academy established in Arlington

Central Plains Academy founded at Estacado in Crosby County as a Quaker school

Della Plain Male and Female Institute opened in Floyd County

East Texas Normal College chartered as a private institution at Cooper, Texas

North Texas Normal College (now North Texas State University) opened at Denton

Texas Female Seminary organized at Weatherford by the Cumberland Presbyterian Church

The University of Texas System School of Nursing established as

PAINTING OF Edmund J. Davis, a Republican Reconstruction Governor of Texas. From the portrait in the Texas State
Capitol Rotunda.

— *Photo by The University of Texas*
Institute of Texas Cultures.

the John Sealy Hospital School for Nurses

Pan-American Railway Company chartered

Pecos River Railroad Company chartered

New Braunfels *Herald* began publication

Midlothian *Visitor* began publication at Midlothian

The *Panola Banner* began publication in Carthage published by G.D. Quest and H.M. Knight

Lake McDonald (later known as Lake Austin) built on Colorado River

Constitutional amendment adopted providing for the Railroad Commission to regulate the railroad industry

The Farmers' Home Improvement Society founded in Colorado County as a farmers organization for negroes

Camp Mabry at Austin established as a summer camp for the Texas Volunteer Guard, a forerunner of the National Guard

Armstrong, Collingsworth, Deaf Smith, and Hall counties organized

February. Marble Falls Alliance University projected at Marble Falls

February 8. Wichita Valley Railway Company chartered

March 20. Sherman, Denison, and Dallas Railway Company chartered

March 24. Fort Worth and Denver Terminal Railway Company chartered

July 17. Swisher County organized

September 16. The first session of Howard Payne College opened

November. Polytechnic College at Fort Worth authorized by the Northwest Texas Annual Conference of the Methodist Episcopal Church, South

December. Synodical College was operating at Gainesville in Cooke County

December 13. Georgetown and Granger Railroad Company chartered

1891

Abilene Baptist College (now Hardin-Simmons University) founded

Second Evangelical Lutheran College established at Brenham

Mineral Wells College established at Mineral Wells

Rice Institute chartered and endowed by the estate of William Marsh Rice

Texas Synodical Female College established at Gainesville by the Presbyterian Church

The 02 Ranch established in Brewster and Presidio counties by W.W. Turney

A second Mashed O Ranch established in Jefferson and Chambers counties by W.P. McFaddin, Jr.

The Spade Ranch established on the high plains by Isaac L. Ellwood

DeKalb and Red River Railroad Company in Bowie County changed from a tram to a common carrier

Hearne and Brazos Railway Company chartered

Name of Kansas and Short Line Railroad Company changed to Tyler Southeastern Railway Company

Kildare and Linden Railway, one of the only two unchartered roads in Texas, began operation

South Galveston and Gulf Shore Railroad Company chartered

Name of Texas Central Railway Company changed to Texas Central Railroad Company

Texas, Louisiana, and Eastern Railroad Company chartered

The *Iconoclast* began publication in Austin by William C. Brann

One of the first rain making efforts occurred in Duval County

Lone Star Salt Company organized by Major Byron Parsons

The Fiesta de San Jacinto observing the battle of San Jacinto officially inaugurated in San Antonio

Foard County, named for Major Robert Foard, created and organized

Sterling County, named for Captain W.S. Sterling, created and organized

The following counties were organized: Castro, Dallam, Dickens, Ector, King, Lubbock, Motley

January 12. Tyler Southeastern Railway chartered

February 9. Hartley County organized

February 12. Texas Legislature granted a pension to Señora Andrea Castanon Candalaria as a survivor of the Alamo

April. Laredo Seminary chartered under the name of Holding Institute

April 13. The Alien Land Law passed during the James Stephen Hogg administration to limit foreign ownership of land

July 7. Crockett County organized

July 29. Velasco Terminal Railway Company (later Houston and Brazos Valley Railway) chartered

August 18. Statewide convention organized of the People's Party

September. North Texas Baptist College opened at Jacksboro under Baptist sponsorship

September 7. Gainesville College opened in Cooke County

November 6. Daughters of the Republic of Texas founded

December. Tin Horn War began along the Mexican border by revolutionaries fighting the regime of Porfirio Diaz of Mexico

December. Northwest Texas Baptist College (later Decatur Baptist College) founded at Decatur

December 11. In *Gunter* v. *Texas Land and Mortgage Company* the Alien Land Law of 1891 was declared unconstitutional on technical grounds

1892

Henry College established at Campbell in Hunt County

Name of North Texas Female College changed to North Texas Female College and Kidd-Key Conservatory of Music

Speer Institute (also known as Ferris Institute) founded at Ferris in Ellis County

Houston Railway Company organized

The Rock Island Railroad System entered Texas with the chartering of the Chicago, Rock Island, and Texas Railway Company

Sabine Pass, Alexandria, and Northwestern Railway Company incorporated at Tyler

The Elisabet Ney Museum built originally as the studio of Elisabet Ney

The first battleship *Texas* launched

Boll weevil brought to Texas from Mexico

Midlothian *Argus* began publication at Midlothian

Name of *Western Baptist* changed to *Baptist Standard*

Amarillo incorporated as a city

The following counties were organized: Briscoe, Borden, Cottle, Kent, Moore, Ward

January 9. Texas Academy of Science organized at the University of Texas

January 18. Trinity, Cameron, and Western Railroad Company chartered

April 6. San Antonio State Hospital opened as Southwestern Lunatic Asylum

April 12. A new Alien Land Law was passed by the Legislature to replace the law of 1891 that had been declared unconstitutional

June 24. North Galveston, Houston, and Kansas City Railroad chartered

July 13. Aransas Harbor Terminal Company incorporated for railroad construction

July 15. Chicago, Rock Island, and Texas Railway Company chartered

August. The Turner Hall Convention resulted from the division in the Democratic Party over national politics

August 16. Name of Car-Stable Convention given to the Democratic State Convention

September. Name of Abilene Baptist College (now Hardin-Simmons University) changed to Simmons College to honor James B. Simmons, a major contributor

October 7. The La Porte, Houston, and Northern Railroad Company incorporated

October 17. Texas and Sabine Valley Railway chartered

1893

Cherokee Academy in San Saba County established

Patroon College opened by Disciples of Christ in Shelby County

Synodical College taken over by the Presbyterian Church

Stephenville College began at Stephenville

West Texas Military Academy founded at San Antonio

Houston and Texas Central Railroad changed to Houston and Texas Railroad Company

Northeastern extension of the Houston and Texas Railroad Company separated as the Texas-Midland Railroad

The *Alamo and San Jacinto Monthly* published by the Alamo Society and the San Jacinto Society at Georgetown

Livestock Sanitary Commission established by the legislature

Sister-Servants of the Holy Ghost and Mary Immaculate founded in San Antonio by Margaret Healey Murphy

February 2. Chicago, Rock Island, and Gulf Railway Company chartered in Texas

February 3. Rio Grande Northern Railroad incorporated

February 28. Sherman, Shreveport, and Southern Railroad Company (originally the East Line and Red River Railroad Company) chartered

March 10. Cane Belt Railroad chartered

March 31. Gulf, Beaumont, and Kansas City Railway Company chartered

April 11. The Sons of the Republic of Texas organized at Richmond

April 14. Sugar Land Railroad Company chartered

July 8. Loving County organized

December 22. San Antonio and Gulf Shore Railway chartered

1894

Adair Normal School at Whitesboro opened

Alexander Institute moved from Kilgore to Jacksonville

Bay View College for girls established at Portland, Texas, by Thomas Marshall Clark

Central College in Sulphur Springs sold to H.N. Eastman and renamed Eastman College

East Texas Baptist Institute established in Cherokee County

Lockney Christian College started by the Church of Christ at Lockney

Mercy Academy, a Catholic institution, established at Stanton in Martin County

Peacock Military Academy established in San Antonio

Rockwall College (also known as Wells College) established at Rockwall

Texas College established at Tyler by the Colored Methodist Episcopal Church

Caro Northern Railway Company with a total of 16½ miles of track chartered

Lake Creek Railway Company chartered

Wichita Falls Railway Company organized

The *Iconoclast* which had failed in August was revived in Waco by William C. Brann

Rolling Stone, a newspaper edited by William Sydney Porter (O. Henry), began publication in Austin

Cotton Palace built in Waco as a hall for fairs and expositions

Charles A. Culberson elected governor of Texas

January 7. Southwestern Junior College organized as Keene Industrial Academy at Keene by the Seventh Day Adventist Church

March 25. A group of men who were a part of Coxey's Army boarded a train in El Paso for Washington, D.C.

March 31. The contingent of Coxey's Army moving through Texas arrived at Longview

May 19. Gulf and Interstate Railway Company started

September. Carr-Burdette College, a school for girls, opened at Sherman under the leadership of Mrs. Mattie F. Carr and the Disciples of Christ

September 6. San Antonio Female College opened at San Antonio

October 29. Name of Galveston Historical Society changed to Texas Historical Society

November 21. Sheriff Royal was killed at Fort Stockton as a part of a feud between Jim Miller and Bud Frazier

1895

Name of Alexander Institute changed to Alexander Collegiate Institute

A Bible College which eventually became Brite College of the Bible organized at Texas Christian University

East Texas Normal College moved to Commerce

Our Lady of the Lake Academy and Normal School established in San Antonio

Westminster College opened in Collin County in the plant of Seven Points College under Methodist supervision

North Galveston, Houston, and Kansas City Railroad incorporated with the La Porte, Houston, and Northern Railroad and called the Galveston, La Porte, and Houston Railway

Name of Rio Grande and Pecos Railroad changed to Rio Grande and Eagle Pass Railroad

Austin Dam and Suburban Railway Company chartered

A weekly publication devoted to politics, society, and the arts, the *Beau Monde,* started in Dallas

Midland *Stock-Reporter* began publication at Midland

Texas State Labor Union organized

Brahman cattle introduced into Texas

January. West Texas Normal and Business College organized at Cherokee in San Saba County

April 4. The so-called Four-Section Act passed to allow sale or lease of public land

April 8. Denison and Pacific Suburban Railway Company chartered

July 18. East Texas Baptist Institute chartered

September. Burleson College, named for Rufus C. Burleson, formally opened in Greenville

October. Discovery of oil began the Corsicana Oil Field and a subsequent oil boom

November 26. Fort Worth Belt Railway Company incorporated

December 25. Add-Ran Christian University moved to Waco

1896

John T. Allen School in Austin established to provide manual training for white boys

Burnetta College sponsored by the Disciples of Christ opened in Johnson County

Rockwall College (also known as Wells College) chartered

Construction began on the Texas State Railroad built by the state

Southwestern Exposition and Fat Stock Show first held at Fort Worth

S.M. Swenson, founder of the SMS Ranches, died

Wonder Cave, (first called Beaver Cave) discovered near San Marcos

January 1. Albert J. Fountain, prominent in El Paso politics, killed in New Mexico

February 19. Texas Presbyterian University chartered at Highland Park, but it never opened

February 21. The Fitzsimmons-Maher heavyweight fight was staged on a sand bar in the Rio Grande by Judge Roy Bean

March 16. Dispute over boundary between Texas and Oklahoma settled by the United States Supreme Court

March 16. The United States Supreme Court ruled that Greer County was not a part of Texas

May. The first issue of *The Texas Magazine* appeared in Austin

May 25. Texas Division of the United Daughters of the Confederacy organized at Victoria

Summer. Camp Ben McCulloch organized in Hays County as a reunion camp for Confederate veterans

June 5. El Paso and Northeastern Railroad Company chartered

July 1. The Sons of Confederate Veterans, the parent organization of the Texas chapter, organized

August 6. The Marshall, Timpson, and Sabine Pass Railroad Company chartered

September 15. A train wreck stunt was staged near Waco by running two locomotives head-on at 90 miles an hour, but it was a disaster when two people were killed

October 10. Union achieved between the Lily-Whites and the regular Republican Party

October 14. Second Clifton Academy opened by Norwegian Lutherans

1897

Add-Ran Jarvis College organized at Thorp Spring in Hood County

Texas Military Institute (different from those in Galveston, Bastrop, Austin, and San Antonio) was in operation at Llano

Toon College established at Terrell

Westminster College in Collin County chartered

Colorado Valley Railroad chartered

Name of Paris, Marshall, and Sabine Pass Railroad changed to Texas Southern Railway

Port Arthur Canal and Dock Company organized to dig a channel from Port Arthur to deep water at Sabine Pass

Texarkana and Fort Smith Railway Company of Texas completed

Texas, Arkansas, and Louisiana Railway built

Fort Crockett, named for David Crockett, built on Galveston Island

Attorney General M.M. Crane filed suit to oust the Waters-Pierce Oil Company from Texas

Hexagon House Hotel built at Mineral Wells for health seekers

April. Foley County abolished

March 2. The organizational meeting of the Texas State Historical Association held at the state capitol

March 9. El Paso Southern Railway Company incorporated

April. Buchel County abolished

May. Texas Federation of Women's Clubs organized at Waco

July. The *Quarterly of the Texas State Historical Association* began publication

August. *The Texas Magazine* published at Dallas

August. Waco *Times-Herald* began publication as a consolidation of the Waco *Morning Times* and the Waco *Herald*

September. The first Amarillo College opened for classes

November. Name of Northwest Texas Baptist College changed to Decatur Baptist College and made a junior college

1898

Clarendon College and University Training School opened in Clarendon as a junior college supported by the Methodist Episcopal Church, South

Elmwood Institute, a preparatory school, established in Hunt County

Goodnight Academy founded by Charles Goodnight and Dr. Marshall McIlhany and later given to the Baptist Church

St. Philip's Normal and Industrial School (later St. Philip's College) founded at San Antonio

Property of Stephenville College transferred to the newly-created John Tarleton College at Stephenville

South Texas Baptist College established at Waller

Tyler Commercial College founded at Tyler

Bohemian, a quarterly literary magazine, founded in Fort Worth by Mrs. Henrie C.L. Gorman

The *Weekly News* began publication at Mexia

Gulf, Beaumont, and Great Northern Railway Company chartered

Moscow, Camden, and San Augustine Railroad built

Pecos and Northern Texas Railway Company chartered

First commerical oil refinery built at Corsicana by J.S. Cullinan

Mercury mining became active by Marfa and Mariposa Mining Company

Landa Park in New Braunfels was in operation

First Church of the Nazarene established in Texas

The Rough Riders (officially the First United States Cavalry Volunteers) trained in San Antonio for service in Cuba in the Spanish-American War

Charles A. Culberson elected to the United States Senate

Bermuda onions first grown commercially in Texas in La Salle County

The **Quien** Sabe brand of the Quien Sabe Ranch registered in Pecos County

Citizen's White Primary organized in Marion County to maintain white supremacy in politics

The **Socialist** Labor Party nominated a candidate for governor for the first time

January 10. Reynolds Presbyterian College opened at Albany

February 26. Texas Branch of the Colonial Dames of America organized and incorporated

April 5. The Austin *Tribune* organized

April 20. Fort San Jacinto on Galveston Island occupied by federal troops

May 10. West Texas Normal and Business College chartered

December 25. J.S. Cullinan Company began operating a refinery at Corsicana

1899

Allen Academy incorporated at Bryan

Texas Society of the Daughters of the American Revolution organized

Control of Burleson College transferred to Baptist State Convention and it was reorganized as a junior college

North Texas Normal College chartered as North Texas State Normal College (now North Texas State University)

Randolph College opened in Lancaster

Legislature authorized the establishment of Southwest Texas Normal School at San Marcos (now Southwest Texas State University)

Texas Holiness University begun at Peniel near Greenville by the Nazarene Church

Name of Galveston, La Porte, and Houston Railway changed to Galveston, Houston, and Northern Railroad

After it was sold the name of the Houston Belt and Magnolia Park Railway Company was rechartered as the Houston, Oaklawn, and Magnolia Park Railway Company

Jefferson and Northwestern Railroad changed from a tram line to a common carrier

Trinity Valley Southern Railroad Company incorporated

Warren and Corsicana Pacific Railroad chartered

Corsicana Petroleum Company organized

Legislature passed first law to regulate oil industry

A TYPICAL steam engine so common in Texas for so many
years.

— Photo from Temple Industries, Diboll, Texas.
Copy from The University of Texas Institute of Texan Cultures.

A **Texas** law passed making labor union membership legal

Texas ranked third as a sugar producing state

February 24. First shipment of refined oil left Corsicana

March 12. Encinal County abolished

March 25. Sabine-Neches Waterway and the Sabine Pass Ship Channel formally opened

March 26. Beaumont Wharf and Terminal Company incorporated

March 30. Galveston, Houston, and Northern Railway Company chartered

June 17-28. The Brazos Flood occurred causing over $9 million in damage and 284 deaths

June 28. Calvert, Waco, and Brazos Valley Railroad Company chartered

July 15. Panhandle and Gulf Railway Company chartered

September. Jacksonville Baptist College at Jacksonville opened for classes supported by the Baptist Missionary Association

September 30. Bexar Archives were transferred by contract to the University of Texas at Austin

October 22. Jaybird Democratic Organization of Fort Bend County organized

1900

Baylor University College of Medicine, now in Houston, was organized in Dallas and was known as the Medical Department of the University of Dallas

John B. Denton College organized at Denton

Kansas City, Mexico, and Orient Railway Company of Texas chartered

Four Sixes Ranch headquarters moved to King County

Meat packing was the sixth ranking industry in the state

Rosenberg Library Association incorporated

The *Daily Texan*, the student newspaper at the University of Texas at Austin, began as a weekly newspaper

The Eagle Lake project completed

Over 16,000 Poles were estimated to be living in Texas

Caverns of Sonora discovered in Sutton County

March 9. St. Louis, San Francisco, and Texas Railway Company chartered

April 21. Washington State Park, named for Washington-on-the-Brazos, had its beginning

June 4. A battle occurred around the courthouse in San Augustine as a part of the Broocks-Border-Wall Feud

July 24. Texas and Louisiana Railroad chartered

July 25. Charter adopted for Dickson Colored Orphanage in Gilmer

August 23. Angelina and Neches River Railroad chartered as a common carrier

Fall. Samuel Huston College, a Methodist school for Negroes, opened at Austin

September 8-9. The "Great Galveston Storm," known as the worst natural disaster in United States history, occurred when a tidal wave swept along by a hurricane inundated Galveston Island

October 9. Texas Southeastern Railroad chartered

November 8. Second Eastern Texas Railroad chartered

December 17. Chicago, Rock Island, and Mexico Railway Company chartered

1901

Legislature created the Texas Industrial Institute and College for white girls

Texas State College for Women created

Tri-State College (first called Inter-State College) opened by Baptist at Texarkana

Timpson Northwestern Railway chartered

Name of Velasco Terminal Railway Company changed to Velasco, Brazos, and Northern Railway Company when it changed ownership

Oil adopted as a fuel by Texas Central Railroad

Batson Oil Field, near Beaumont, opened

The George A. Burts Refining Company organized

Abilene State Hospital established by Twenty-Seventh Legislature

City of Galveston received a new charter that established the commission form of government

Meat packing plants opened in Fort Worth by Swift and Company and Armor and Company

Construction completed on the dam that created Lake Wichita

A Mormon colony established at Kelsey in Upshur County

O Bar O Ranch established by J. S. Bilby

Hutchinson and Schleicher counties organized

January 4. Dickson Colored Orphanage opened and dedicated

January 10. Lucas Gusher came in at Spindletop near Beaumont

January 14. Orange and Northwestern Railway Company converted to a common carrier

February 4. Red River, Texas, and Southern Railway Company chartered

February 12. Calvert, Waco, and Brazos Valley Railroad Company merged with International-Great Northern Railroad

February 28. Texas Short Line Railway Company chartered

March. Joseph Stephen Cullinan incorporated the Texas Fuel Company at Beaumont

March 7. The bluebonnet adopted as the state flower

April 4. El Paso Terminal Railroad Company chartered

May. J.M. Guffey Petroleum Company organized

June 21. Choctaw, Oklahoma, and Texas Railroad Company chartered

July. The Yellow House Ranch began by George Washington Littlefield in Lamb, Hockley, Bailey, and Cochran counties

July 2. Blackwell, Enid, and Texas Railway Company chartered

July 6. Southern Pacific Terminal Company incorporated

October 14. Houston *Chronicle* began publication

December 26. Oklahoma City and Texas Railroad Company chartered

1902

Add-Ran Christian University at Waco changed its name to Texas Christian University

Trinity University moved from Tehuacana to Waxahachie

Westminster College moved from Collin County to Tehuacana

El Paso and Southwestern Railroad Company chartered

The Northeast Texas Railway Company chartered

Trinity and Brazos Valley Railway Company chartered by E.M. House

Farmers' Educational and Co-operative Union of America, usually known as the Farmers' Union, founded at Emory, Texas, by Newt Gresham

Gray County organized

April. A new charter for the Texas Fuel Company issued under the name of the Texas Company

May 3. Chicago, Rock Island, and Gulf Railway Company chartered

May 18. Goliad was hit by a tornado that killed 114 people

June 3. Dallas, Cleburne, and Southwestern Railway Company chartered

June 9. Texas Library Association organized at Austin

July 12. Quanah, Acme, and Pacific Railroad chartered as the Acme, Red River, and Northern Railroad

September. Hereford College and Industrial School opened at Hereford

September 24. Texas Presbyterian College opened at Milford

October 1. Austin Presbyterian Theological Seminary opened

December 5. Granger, Georgetown, Austin, and San Antonio Railway Company chartered

December 31. White Man's Union Association organized in Jackson County to maintain white supremacy in politics

1903

Gunter Bible College started by the Church of Christ

San Antonio Philosophical and Theological Seminary (now Oblate College of the Southwest) opened

Baylor Hospital in Dallas established by Texas Baptists

The Pasteur Institute of Texas organized

The state Department of Public Health established

Texas legislature provided funds for public schools to teach vocational education

The Log of a Cowboy by Andy Adams published

Livingston and Southeastern Railway Company chartered

Various Rock Island lines consolidated under the name Chicago, Rock Island, and Gulf Railway Company

Wichita Falls and Oklahoma Railway Company began construction

Dallas Art Association founded

State Topics, A Journal of the People began publication at Austin

Name of *Street's Weekly* changed to *Holland's Magazine*

Reagan County, named for John H. Reagan, created and organized

Lynn County organized

January 12. St. Louis, Brownsville, and Mexico Railway Company chartered

February. Equal Suffrage League organized at Houston as the first sustained movement for women's suffrage

May 12. The "Eyes of Texas," the official song of the University of Texas at Austin, first performed at a varsity minstrel show

August 8. Beaumont, Sour Lake, and Port Arthur Traction Company chartered to build an electric interurban train

September. Emerson College at Campbell, Texas, opened

September. Texas State College for Women opened at Denton

September. Gunter Bible College, a junior college operated by the Church of Christ, opened in Grayson County

September 9. Southwest Texas Normal School (now Southwest Texas State University) opened

December. Texas Womans Suffrage Association organized

1904

Canadian Academy, a Baptist school, established in Canadian, Texas

Peach River and Gulf Railway Company became a common carrier

Texas and Gulf Railroad Company organized

Abilene State Hospital opened to receive patients

Temple Sanitarium (now Scott and White Memorial Hospital) established at Temple

The first training of architects began in Texas with the establishment of a department at Texas A & M College

First commercial grove of grapefruit trees planted

Petrolia Oil Field opened in Clay County

The Holiness Church of Christ and the Independent Holiness Church merged at a meeting at Rising Star

June. Rosenberg Library opened in Galveston

June 30. Beaumont, Sour Lake, and Western Railway Company chartered

July 5. Terry County organized

October 1. Southwestern Christian College opened at Denton in the plant of John B. Denton College acquired by the Church of Christ

November 11. Jasper and Eastern Railroad chartered

1905

Butler College established as Texas Baptist Academy in Tyler by the East Texas Baptist Association for black youth

Name of *Hereford College and Industrial School changed to Pan-Handle Christian College*

St. Anthony Seminary established at San Antonio by the Missionary Oblates of Mary Immaculate

State Dental College chartered in Dallas as a private institution

Texas Baptist University established in Dallas

Texas Dental College established at Houston

The University of Texas Dental Branch at Houston established as a private institution

Beaumont and Saratoga Transportation Company chartered

Houston Belt and Terminal Railway Company chartered

Nueces Valley, Rio Grande, and Mexico Railway chartered

Wichita Valley Railroad Company chartered

Juliette Fowler Homes for Orphans and Aged came under the jurisdiction of the Disciples of Christ

Name of the Asylum for the Blind changed to Blind Institute

First Mennonite Church in Texas founded at Tuleta

A state banking system under the leadership of Thomas B. Love was established

The office of adjutant general established by the legislature

Terrell Election Law provided for direct primary elections

Motion pictures began to be shown in Texas theaters

Terrell County, named for Alexander Watkins Terrell, created and organized

State Tax Board (usually called the Intangible Tax Board) established by the legislature

Irrigation districts first authorized by the legislature

January. Rosenberg Library in Galveston opened a branch for

Negroes, the first of its kind in the United States

January 7. The first large strike made in the Humble Oil Field in Harris County

January 25. Texas Legislature authorized the purchase of all the Alamo property and its delivery to the Daughters of the Republic of Texas

April 15. Eight-Section Act passed by the legislature that amended the sale and lease of public lands

April 20. North Texas University School (later Wesley College) organized by the Methodist Episcopal Church, South at Terrell

June 22. Beaumont and Great Northern Railway Company chartered

August 29. Galveston Terminal Railway Company chartered

October 24. Gaines County organized

1906

San Marcos Academy established at San Marcos by the Baptist Church

Stamford College founded by the Methodist Church at Stamford

State Dental College opened for students

Shreveport, Houston, and Gulf Railroad Company chartered

Trinity Valley and Northern Railway Company incorporated

Wichita Falls and Northwestern Railway Company organized

Burr's Ferry, Browndell, and Chester Railroad built near Aldredge, Texas

Charles William Post established Post City and began a utopian communal effort in West Texas

Oil production from the Powell Oil Field in Navarro County reached its peak

Commercial production of peanuts began in Texas

Statewide association of chamber of commerce executives organized

The Farmers' Improvement Agricultural College established at Wolfe City by the Farmers' Home Improvement Society

The Socialist Party organized in Texas

Spur Ranch established in West Texas

Texas Presbyterian Home and School for Orphans opened near Itasca

Two Unitarian Churches existed in Texas

Church of Christ broke away from the Disciples of Christ (Christian Church)

Proposal made to create four legislatures in Texas under one governor

The song, "Eyes of Texas" with lyrics by John L. Sinclair, sung for the first time as a prank

February 1. The present-day Fort Worth *Star-Telegram* originated

September 11. Abilene Christian College (now Abilene Christian University) opened

October 2. Trinity Lutheran College opened at Round Rock

1907

Central Plains College and Conservatory of Music built in Plainview by the Holiness Church

Meridian Training School (later Meridian Junior College) incorporated

Sabinal Christian College started by the Church of Christ

The first University of Dallas opened as a Catholic college

Abilene and Northern Railway Company between Stamford and Abilene opened

Southwestern Railway Company chartered

Name of Velasco, Brazos, and Northern Railroad changed to Houston and Brazos Valley Railroad

Wichita Falls and Southern Railway Company chartered

The Department of Agriculture was established as a separate state department

Board to Calculate the Ad Valorem Tax Rate (also called the automatic tax board) established by the legislature

Pueblo ruins in the Texas Panhandle first explored by Professor T. L. Eyerly, Floyd V. Studer, and others

Houston Baptist Hospital founded

The Texas branch of the Anti-Saloon League organized

The State Board of Pharmacy created

The San Jacinto Battleground Commission created

The "Galveston Plan" or "Galveston Movement" began by which about 10,000 Jews from eastern Europe immigrated to the United States through Texas

The Neiman-Marcus Company founded in Dallas

Garza, Parmer and Yoakum counties organized

January. Gulf Oi Corporation formed

February 4. Stephenville North and South Texas Railway Company chartered

May 14. *Wichita Daily Times* published first evening edition

May 30. The Imperial Valley Railroad chartered

September. Stamford College opened

September 10. Sabinal Christian College founded in Uvalde County

1908

Name of Pan-Handle Christian College changed to Hereford College (originally Hereford College and Industrial School)

Name of Texas College at Tyler changed to Phillips University

Estacado and Gulf Railroad Company chartered

Groveton, Lufkin, and Northern Railway Company chartered

Name of Texas Southern Railway changed to the Marshall and East Texas Railway Company

Confederate Woman's Home opened

Westminster Encampment of the Presbyterian Church chartered at Kerrville

The Church of the Nazarene began as a national church at Pilot Point, Texas, when a merger of several Holiness churches occurred

Texas Business Men's Association founded

A few descendants of the Pascagoula Indians found living in Polk County

Jewish *Herald-Voice* began publication at Houston

June 20. Lamb County organized

October 1. Roscoe, Snyder, and Pacific Railway Company chartered

November 2. Gulf Texas, and Western Railroad Company chartered

November 17. The Artesian Belt Railroad chartered

November 17. San Antonio Southern Railway Company (originally the Artesian Belt Railroad company) chartered

1909

Baylor University took total responsibility for the Medical Department of the University of Dallas

Bryan Baptist Academy established in the plant of Texas Woman's College

Central Nazarene College chartered in Hamlin

Clebarro College at Cleburne started by the Church of Christ

Midland Christian College established in Midland as a junior college by the Disciples of Christ

Name of North Texas University School at Terrell changed to Wesley College

Port Arthur College built and endowed by John Warne Gates at Port Arthur

The Acme Tap Railroad Company, the shortest railroad in Texas at 1.51 miles, was organized and constructed

Bartlett-Florence Railway Company chartered; name changed later to Bartlett and Western Railroad

Crystal City and Uvalde Railroad Company (later known as the

San Antonio, Uvalde, and Gulf Railroad Company) chartered

Llano Estacado Railroad chartered, but it was sold to the Panhandle and Santa Fe Railroad before it was completed

Nacogdoches and Southeastern Railroad Company chartered

Port Isabel and Rio Grande Valley Railway chartered

Name of Quanah, Acme, and Pacific Railroad changed to Acme, Red River, and Northern Railroad

Stamford and Northwestern Railway Company chartered

Timpson and Henderson Railway Company succeeded the Timpson Northwestern Railway

Amarillo *News* founded

Texas Spur at Spur, Texas, established

Bureau of Labor Statistics established

Legislative authorization provided for the creation of navigation districts

Legislature authorized the establishment of levee improvement districts

Bureau of Economic Geology established as a research bureau of the University of Texas at Austin

Texas Gulf Sulphur Company organized to develop Big Hill Sulphur Dome in Matagorda County

John Sealy Company purchased the Navarro Refining Company and the Security Oil Company

Curtain Club organized at the University of Texas by Stark Young

Construction completed on Lake Randall in Grayson County

The Elisabet Ney Museum in Austin opened to the public

Dallas Free Public Art Gallery (now Dallas Museum of Fine Arts) opened

Texas Folklore Society originally founded

Texas State Library and Historical Commission established

January 13. Abilene and Southern Railway Company chartered to run between Ballinger and Hamlin

January 29. Paris and Mt. Pleasant Railway Company chartered

March 9. The Asherton and Gulf Railway Company chartered

April 1. Construction of the Rio Grande bridge begun by Brownsville and Matamoros Bridge Company

April 2. Concho, San Saba, and Llano Valley Railroad incorporated

April 24. Waters-Pierce Oil Company paid a fine and interest totalling $1,8098,483.30 in settlement of the Waters-Pierce Case

May. The *Pitchfork,* a monthly magazine, moved to Dallas

May 28. Pecos Valley Southeren Railway Company chartered

September. Meridian Training School (later Meridian Junior College) became affiliated with the Methodist Episcopal Church, South

September 15. Clebarro College moved from Denton to Cleburne

SCENE OF students at Fredericksburg College, founded by the German Methodist Church in 1876.

— *Photo from Kilman Studio, Fredericksburg.*
Copy from The University of Texas Institute of Texan Cultures.

October. *The Texas Magazine* published at Houston

October 19. The Texas Congress of Parents and Teachers originated in Dallas

December 29. The Texas Folklore Society formally organized

1910

Southwestern Baptist Theological Seminary established at Fort Worth

Thorp Spring Christian College directed by the Disciples of Christ opened at Thorp Spring in the plant of Add-Ran Jarvis College

West Texas State College opened at Canyon under the name, West Texas State Normal College

Bryan and College Station Interurban Railway Company constructed

Crosbyton-South Plains Railroad built

Wichita Falls and Wellington Railway Company was in operation

Hunter's Magazine began publication in Carlsbad, Texas

Randall County News started in Canyon by C.W. Warwick

The University Interscholastic League had its beginning as the Debating League of Texas High Schools

Name of Texas Presbyterian Home and School for Orphans changed to Southwestern Presbyterian Home and School for Orphans

Oscar B. Colquitt elected governor as an anti-prohibitionist

Meat packing was the state's most important industry

Construction began on San Estaban Lake

Andrews, Upton, and Winkler counties organized

January 29. Brownwood North and South Railway Company chartered

March 17. Temple-Northwestern Railway Company chartered

March 28. Missouri, Oklahoma, and Gulf Railway Company of Texas chartered

April 19-20. Texas Industrial Congress organized at San Antonio as a type of chamber of commerce

June 16. Central Plains College and Conservatory of Music in Plainview sold by the Holiness Church to the Methodist Church which changed the name to Seth Ward College

June 25. Caddo Lake came under federal government jurisdiction

September 1. Lowrey-Phillips School opened in Amarillo

September 27. Wayland Baptist College, founded by Dr. J.H. Wayland, opened at Plainview

1911

Central Nazarene College opened at Hamlin

Sam Houston Normal Institute became a junior college

Pentecostal Church of the Nazarene adopted Texas Holiness University and changed its name to Peniel University

111

Saint Ignatius Academy became Our Lady of Victory College

Texas Mexican Industrial Institute organized at Kingsville by the Presbyterian Church

The Debating League of Texas High Schools became the Debating and Declamation League of Texas Schools

The Farmers' Bank established at Waco by the Farmers' Home Improvement Society

Construction completed on White Rock Dam that created White Rock Lake in Dallas County

One of the first successful paper plants established at Orange by Edward H. Mayo

C.W. Post began rainmaking activities near Post, Texas

Studies in English began publication at the University of Texas

Name of the state reformatory at Gatesville changed to State Institution for the Training of Juveniles

Port Bolivar Iron Ore Railway built

The following counties were created: Brooks, named for James Abijah Brooks; Culberson, named for David B. Culberson; Jim Wells named for James B. Wells; Willacy, named for John G. Willacy

February. Humble Oil Company chartered in Texas

February 16. Dispute over the western boundary of Texas Panhandle with New Mexico settled by Congress

April. Texas Fine Arts Association organized

April 1. The oil boom known as the Electra Oil Field began

April 4. Methodist Church took control of West Texas Normal and Business College and operated it as Cherokee Junior College until 1921

April 8. The first formal meeting of the Texas Folklore Society held in Austin

April 24. Magnolia Petroleum Company founded as a joint stock association

September. Following a fire in Waco, Texas Christian University relocated on a permanent campus in Fort Worth

September. The Houston *Press* founded

1912

Canadian Academy closed

Evangelical Lutheran College (later Texas Lutheran College) moved from Brenham to Seguin

Our Lady of the Lake College became a two-year college

Rice Institute opened for instruction

Texas Wesleyan College Academy opened at Austin

Toon College at Terrell became Terrell University School

Brownsville Street and Interurban Railroad Company (later the

San Benito and Rio Grande Valley Railway Company) chartered

Name of Crystal City and Uvalde Railroad Company changed to San Antonio, Uvalde, and Gulf Railroad Company

Greenville and Whitewright Northern Traction Company chartered

Lufkin, Hemphill, and Gulf Railway chartered

Riviera Beach and Western Railroad built

San Benito and Rio Grande Valley Interurban Railway Company chartered

San Benito and Rio Grande Valley Railway Company chartered

Benjamin H. Carroll, Jr. owned, published, and edited *The Stylus,* a weekly magazine in Houston

Name of *The Quarterly of the Texas State Historical Association* changed to *The Southwestern Historical Quarterly*

Texas Haymakers Association had been formed

The first Turkey Trot, an annual festival, held at Cuero

The Texas Land and Development Company organized at Plainview

Medina Lake in Bandera and Medina counties completed

Brooks, Culberson, and Jim Wells counties organized

March 16. The Union Terminal Company of Dallas chartered

May 2. San Antonio Belt and Terminal Railway Company chartered

July 4. The Colony No. 1, Carlsbad, Texas, (later McKnight State Sanatorium) opened in Tom Green County for white tuberculous patients

August. The Littlefield Lands Company organized by George Washington Littlefield

Fall. Texas Mexican Industrial Institute at Kingsville opened

October 23. College of Marshall (later East Texas Baptist College) chartered

1913

Carlton College of Bonham joined with Carr-Burdette College in Sherman

Jarvis Christian College opened at Hawkins supported by the Disciples of Christ

Weatherford College became the property of the Methodist Church

Name of State Institution for the Training of Juveniles changed to State Juvenile Training School

Gainesville State School for Girls established for delinquent and dependent white girls

Name of Colony No. 1 changed to State Tuberculosis Sanatorium (later McKnight State Sanatorium)

Board of Water Engineers established by the legislature

First oil wells discovered near Burkburnett in Wichita County

Texas Chapter of the American Institute of Architects founded

Industrial Accident Board established by the legislature

Legislature passed a new law allowing voter approved irrigation districts

Jim Hogg County named for James Stephen Hogg, created and organized

Real County, named for Justus Real, created

Baptist Standard was acquired by the Baptist General Convention

La Prensa, a Spanish language newspaper, began in San Antonio

February 27. Kleberg County, named for Robert Justus Kleberg, created

March 6. Albert Sidney Burleson appointed postmaster general by President Woodrow Wilson

May 7. Impoundment of water began in Medina Lake in Medina and Bandera counties

May 29. Construction of Gulf Intracoastal Waterway below Galveston completed

June 27. Kleberg County organized

September. Hockaday School established in Dallas by Ela Hockaday

September 24. The *Daily Texan* at the University of Texas at Austin became a daily newspaper

November 4. League of Texas Municipalities formed

November 23. The Inman Christian Center (originally the Mexican Christian Institute) permanently located at San Antonio by the Christian Church (Disciples of Christ)

1914

Name of Alexander Collegiate Institute changed to Alexander College College

Name of Greenville and Whitewright Northern Traction Company changed to Greenville and Northwestern Railway Company

Panhandle and Santa Fe Railway Company organized

Uvalde and Northern Railroad chartered

Texas School Journal and *Texas School Magazine* consolidated

The Cattlemen established by the Texas and Southwestern Cattle Raisers' Association

James E. Ferguson elected governor

Thomas Watt Gregory appointed attorney general by President Woodrow Wilson

Major George W. Littlefield established the Littlefield Southern History Fund

Texas Co-operative Poultry Producers' Assocation organized

Fannin Battleground State Historic Site near Goliad in Goliad County acquired by the Board of Control

Texas Forest Service originated out of the Texas Forest Association

Texas Engineering Experiment Station established

Bayland Orphans' Home Association name changed to Bayland Orphans' Home for Boys and no longer accepted girls

Federal Reserve Bank established in Dallas

Love Field established at Dallas as an army airport and aviation training center

Meachem Field established at Fort Worth as an army air base

March 12. The second battleship *Texas* commissioned

April. Benjamin H. Carroll, Jr. appointed United States Consul to Venice, Italy, by President Woodrow Wilson

April 1. The Dallas *Journal* established by the publishers of the Dallas *Morning News*

May 1. William Theodotus Capers consecrated as bishop-coadjutor of the Diocese of West Texas of the Protestant Episcopal Church

May 1. Rio Grande, El Paso, and Santa Fe Railroad chartered

May 6. The Southwest Conference for athletics temporarily organized

May 31. The first issue of the Austin *American* published

Fall. State School of Mines and Metallurgy opened at El Paso

September. Texas Woman's College opened at Fort Worth on the same campus with Polytechnic College

September 14. Houston Ship Channel completed

September 21. Texas Military College, a high school and junior college, founded at Terrell by Louis C. Perry

December 8. Southwest Conference formally organized

1915

Sam Houston Normal Institute became a four year college

Crosbyton-South Plains Railroad purchased by the Santa Fe and name changed to South Plains and Santa Fe Railroad Company

The Trail Drivers Association organized to perpetuate the memory of the old cattle trail drivers

Name of Blind Insitute changed to Texas School for the Blind

Hunter's Frontier Magazine began publication at Melvin, Texas

Texas Review published at the University of Texas

February 11. Texas Legislature passed legislation that involved the "chicken salad case" that became involved in the impeachment charges against James E. Ferguson

March 2. Legislature created three new normal colleges, one of which was to be named for Stephen F. Austin

May. First athletic event of the Southwest Conference, a track and field meet, held at the University of Texas

September 22. Southern Methodist University opened in Dallas

1916

Southwestern Union College at Keene founded under the name Southwestern Junior College by the Seventh-day Adventist Church

Property donated to the state for Mother Neff State Recreation Park near Moody in Coryell County

Lake Worth on the West Fork of the Trinity River completed in Tarrant County

Pink bollworm entered Texas from Mexico

James E. Ferguson reelected governor

January 16. Midland and Northwestern Railway Company chartered

July 25. North Texas and Santa Fe Railway incorporated

August. Goose Creek Oil Field began

August 18. A hurricane hit Corpus Christi killing twenty people and inflicting $1.5 million in damages

August 29. Texas State Council of Defense created at the request of Secretary of War Newton D. Baker

October. Name of *State Topics, A Journal of the People* changed to *Texas Weekly Review*

November. Association of Texas Colleges, formerly a section of the Texas State Teachers Association, created as a separate organization

1917

College of Marshall opened

Name of Peniel University changed to Peniel College

The University of Texas at Arlington started under the name Grubbs Vocational College

Barron Field established in Tarrant County to train Canadian flyers

Brooks Air Force Base established near San Antonio

Camp Bullis, named for John L. Bullis, established near San Antonio

Camp Travis at San Antonio established and named for William B. Travis

Ellington Field (later Ellington Air Force Base) established near Houston

East Texas and Gulf Railway in Tyler County became a common carrier

116

Gulf and Northern Railroad Company chartered

Name of Texas Pacific Coal Company at Thurber changed to Texas Pacific Coal and Oil Company

Water improvement districts authorized by the legislature

Texas Legislature declared that oil pipelines were common carriers and placed them under the regulation of the Railroad Commission

Texas State Highway Department established by the legislature

Wichita Falls State Hospital established by the legislature

State legislature passed Pink Bollworm Act to control the insect

Construction completed on Lake Balmorhea

Sweet Home Colored School was in operation in Guadalupe County as an industrial training school

Texas Outlook, official publication of the Texas State Teachers Association, began publication

Bailey County organized

February. Hudspeth County, named for Claude Benton Hudspeth, created

February 20. Property of John Tarleton College transferred to the state and John Tarleton Agricultural College established as a branch of the Agricultural and Mechanical College of Texas

March. East Texas Normal College became a state supported institution

April 4. Legislature recreated two normal colleges, one to be named for Stephen F. Austin

April 4. Sul Ross State Normal College (now Sul Ross State University) created

May. Construction began on Kelly Air Force Base in San Antonio

May 10. First meeting of the Texas State Council of Defense held in Dallas

May 14. Legal status given to the Texas State Council of Defense by the legislature

May 15. Leon Springs First Officers Training Camp opened in Bexar County

June 26. First post of the Veterans of Foreign Wars established in Texas at San Antonio

July. Dayton-Goose Creek Railroad chartered

July 18. Camp MacArthur, named for General Arthur MacArthur, established near Waco

July 18. The Thirty-Sixth Division, composed mostly of Texas National Guard troops, organized to fight in France

July 21. Governor James E. Ferguson indicted by Travis County grand jury

July 24. Construction on Camp Logan near Houston began

August. Call Field, named for Loren H. Call, established as a

World War I air base near Wichita Falls

August 23. A riot occurred in Houston between local police and black soldiers from Camp Logan that resulted in martial law being declared in Houston

August 25. The Ninetieth Division, also known as the "Tough 'Ombres" or the "Alamo" Division, activated at Camp Travis, Texas

October 2. Name of Camp Funston near San Antonio changed to Camp Stanley and operated as an ammunition storage depot

October 21. Ranger, Desdemona, and Breckenridge Oil Fields began to boom

October 31. The Austin State School was opened to care for feeble minded children

November 8. *Ferguson Forum,* the political newspaper of James E. Ferguson, began publication

December 26. Fredericksburg and Northern Railway Company chartered

1918

State Dental College at Dallas puchased by Baylor University and became Baylor University College of Dentistry

Name of Phillips University at Tyler changed back to Texas College

Southwest Texas Normal School (now Southwest Texas State University) became a senior college and name was changed to Southwest Texas State Normal College

Westmoorland College began operation in the plant of San Antonio Female College under Methodist sponsorship

Bryan and Central Texas Interurban constructed

Construction began on the dam on Elm Creek that later created Lake Abilene

West Texas Today began publication as the official organ of the West Texas Chamber of Commerce

Camp Holland near Valentine built to protect the population from Mexican bandits

Southwestern Political Science Association (now Southwestern Social Science Association) established at the University of Texas at Austin

January 15. West Columbia Oil Field brought in on the Gulf coast

January 29. Brooks Air Force Base near San Antonio occupied

February 28. Texas ratified the eighteenth amendment that provided for total prohibition

March 26. Governor W.P. Hobby signed a bill giving women the right to vote in all primary elections and in all nominating conventions

July. Hull Oil Field opened in Liberty County

July 29. The success of the well known as "Fowler's Folly" began the oil boom at Burkburnett

September 4. San Antonio *Evening News* began publication

September 14. Barber's Hill Oil Field in Chambers County opened

December. The West Texas Chamber of Commerce founded in Fort Worth

December 4. Cisco and Northeastern Railway Company chartered

1919

Eastland, Wichita Falls, and Gulf Railroad Company built

Hockaday School in Dallas chartered as Miss Hockaday's School for Girls

Name of North Texas Female College and Kidd-Key Conservatory of Music changed to Kidd-Key College

Our Lady of the Lake College became a four-year institution

State School of Mines and Metallurgy at El Paso became the College of Mines and Metallurgy and a branch of the University of Texas

The Waco State Home established by the legislature at Waco under the name, State Home for Dependent and Neglected Children

Water supply districts authorized by the legislature

The State Board of Control established

The Texas Department of the American Legion organized at San Antonio

First convention of the West Texas Chamber of Commerce held at Mineral Wells

The pecan chosen by the legislature to be the official state tree

Rusk State Hospital opened at Rusk for the mentally ill

Soldiers and Sailors Moratorium Law passed by the Legislature to protect property of servicemen in World War I

Cattle breeders crossed Shorthorns with Brahmans to begin the process that resulted in the Santa Gertrudis breed

The Benedictine Sisters, an Italian order, first arrived in Texas

January 1. The *Peoples Press*, a labor newspaper, began publication at Port Arthur

February. West Texas Chamber of Commerce chartered

April. Texas Chamber of Commerce formed, but was dissolved four years later

June 20. Motley County Railroad chartered

June 23. Legislature ratified the federal woman's suffrage amendment

September 23. Abilene Christian College (now Abilene Christian University) became a four-year senior college

September 26. Wichita Falls, Ranger, and Fort Worth Railroad Company chartered

119

"THE CAPITOL at Austin in 1870." Engraving from Homer S. Thrall, *Pictorial History of Texas* (1879). The building burned in November 1881.

— *Photo from The University of Texas Institute of Texan Cultures.*

November. The first Little Theatre in Texas, the Green Mask Players, founded at Houston

1920

Name of East Texas Baptist Institute at Rusk changed to Rusk Baptist College

Sacred Heart Scholasticate separated from San Antonio Philosophical and Theological Seminary and moved to Castroville

Fort Ramirez, established in Live Oak County at an unknown date, was in ruins

Veterans Administration Hospital, Legion Branch, established at Kerrville by the Texas American Legion

The Texas American Legion Auxiliary organized

Dallas Little Theatre founded

An early radio station, WRR, began broadcasting from Dallas

Southwestern Social Science Quarterly begun as the official publication of the Southwestern Social Science Association at Austin

The Morton Salt Company absorbed most of the small companies at the salt deposits at Grand Saline

Texas Industrial Commission created

Summer. The first Texas Farm Bureau organized

June 14. Sul Ross State Normal College (now Sul Ross State University) opened at Alpine

September. Construction completed on the original dam that created Lake Mineral Wells

November 15. Name of Meridian Training School changed to Meridian Junior College

MIRIAM AMANDA FERGUSON, Texas first woman governor.

— Courtesy Austin-Travis County Collection

Amarillo College, 1897
Amarillo *News*, 1909
American Institute of Architects, Texas Chapter of, 1913
American Legion Auxiliary, Texas Division of, 1920
American Legion, Texas Department of, 1919
American Revolution, 1832
Amos Wright, 1833
Anachorema Indians, 1687
Anadarko Indians, 1854
Anahuac, Texas, 1756
Anahuac Disturbances, 1835
Anao Indians, 1691
Anathagua Indians, 1748
Anchimo Indians, 1684
Anchose Indians, 1748
Anderson, Texas, 1846, 1852
Anderson, Kenneth Lewis, 1846
Anderson County, 1835, 1846, 1856
Andrew Female Academy, 1853
Andrews, Richard, 1876
Andrews County, 1876, 1910
Angelina County, 1846
Angelina and Neches River Railroad, 1900
Angelina River, 1846
Anglo-Texan Convention, 1840
Anna Judson Female Institute, 1859
Annaho Indians, 1687
Annexation of Texas, 1836, 1837, 1838, 1839, 1844, 1845, 1846
Anti-Quaker, 1842
Anti-Saloon League, Texas Branch of, 1907
Apache Indians, 1675, 1732, 1852
Apapax Indians, 1748
Aranama College, 1854
Aranama Indians, 1722
Aransas County, 1871
Aransas Harbor Terminal Company, 1872
Arcahomo Indians, 1737
Archer, 1840
Archer County, 1858, 1862, 1880
Archer, Branch T., 1858
Architecture, 1904, 1913
Archives, 1850, 1878

Archive War, 1842
Arcos Buenos Indians, 1693
Arcos Pordidos Indians, 1693
Arcos Tirados Indians, 1693
Arcos Tuertos Indians, 1684
Argyle Hotel, 1859
Ariel, 1829
Arihuman Indians, 1683
Arista, Mariano, 1842
Arkansas, 1813, 1862, 1863
Arlington, Texas, 1841, 1890
Armistice, 1843
Armour and Company, 1901
Armstrong County, 1876, 1890
Arredondo, Joaquín de, 1813
Arsenals, 1858
Art Organizations, 1903
Artesian Belt Railroad, 1908
Asen Arcos Indians, 1684
Asherton and Gulf Railway Company, 1909
Assassinations, 1837
Association of Noblemen, 1842, 1844
Association of Texas Colleges, 1916
Asylum for the Blind, 1856, 1905
Asylum for the Deaf, 1856, 1857
Atascosa County, 1856
Atayo Indians, 1528
Athens *Bulletin*, 1873
Athens *Review*, 1885
Athletic Organizations, 1914, 1915
Atia Indians, 1748
Atiasnogue Indians, 1748
Atlantic and Pacific Railroad Company, 1854
Austin, 1840
Austin, Moses, 1761, 1821
Austin, Stephen F., 1793, 1821, 1829, 1834, 1835, 1836, 1915, 1917
Austin, Arkansas, 1862
Austin, Texas, 1709, 1836, 1837, 1840, 1841, 1842, 1843, 1845, 1846, 1848, 1849, 1851, 1852, 1853, 1856, 1857, 1858, 1861, 1866, 1867, 1868, 1870, 1871, 1872, 1873, 1874, 1875, 1877, 1878, 1880, 1881, 1883, 1884, 1885, 1887, 1889, 1890, 1891, 1894, 1896, 1897, 1902, 1903, 1909, 1911, 1912
Austin *American*, 1914

Austin *City Gazette*, 1839
Austin College, 1849, 1878
Austin County, 1718, 1836, 1837
Austin Dam and Suburban Railway Company, 1895
Austin Female Academy, 1850
Austin Female Collegiate Institute, 1852
Austin Lyceum, 1840
Austin and Northwestern Railroad Company, 1881
Austin Presbyterian Theological Seminary, 1902
Austin School of Theology, 1884
Austin State Hospital, 1861
Austin State School, 1917
Austin *Statesman*, 1871
Austin Teachers Association, 1879, 1880
Austin *Tribune*, 1898
Automatic Tax Board, 1907

B

Bacon, Sumner, 1829
Bailey, Peter J., 1876
Bailey County, 1876, 1889, 1901, 1917
Baird, R.A., 1873
Bajunero Indians, 1684
Baker, Newton D., 1916
Balcones Escarpment, 1887
Ballinger, Texas, 1684
Banco Nacional de Tejas, 1822
Bandera, Texas, 1854
Bandera County, 1856, 1862, 1912, 1913
Bandera Pass, Battle of, 1720, 1842
Bands of Hope, 1870
Banks, 1822, 1838, 1847, 1865, 1905
Baptist Church, 1856, 1860, 1861, 1865, 1867, 1898, 1906
Baptist General Association of Texas, 1886
Baptist General Convention, 1886, 1913
Baptist Missionary Association, 1899
Baptist News, 1888
Baptist Standard, 1892, 1913
Baptist State Convention, 1848, 1865, 1886, 1899

Baptist Training Union, 1888
Baptist, 1829, 1837, 1841, 1848, 1853, 1854, 1856, 1858, 1860, 1862, 1865, 1866, 1867, 1869, 1870, 1872, 1875, 1876, 1878, 1881, 1886, 1888, 1889, 1891, 1892, 1894, 1895, 1897, 1899, 1901, 1903, 1904, 1907, 1909, 1912, 1913
Bar Associations, 1882
Barbed Wire, 1879
Barber's Hill Oil Field, 1918
Barksdale, Texas, 1762
Barrett, Lynis T., 1866
Barrio Junco y Espriella, Pedro del, 1748
Barron Field, 1917
Bartlett and Western Railroad, 1909
Bartlett-Condé Compromise, 1850
Bartlett-Florence Railway Company, 1909
Baseball, 1887
Bastrop, Baron Felipe Enrique Neri de, 1836
Bastrop, Texas, 1868, 1870, 1897
Bastrop Academy, 1851, 1853
Bastrop County, 1836, 1837
Bastrop Military Institute, 1858, 1868
Bastrop and Taylor Railway Company, 1886
Bata Indians, 1691
Bates, W.H., 1877
Batson Oil Field, 1901
Battle Creek Fight, 1838
Battle of Agua Dulce Creek, 1836
Battle of Alcantra, 1839
Battle of Brushy Creek, 1839
Battle of Coleto, 1836
Battle of Concepción, 1835
Battle of the Cottonwoods, 1839
Battle of Dove Creek, 1865
Battle of Galveston, 1862
Battle of Gonzales, 1835
Battle of Hynes Bay, 1852
Battle of Jones Creek, 1824
Battle of Mansfield, 1864
Battle of the Medina River, 1813
Battle of Nacogdoches, 1832
Battle of the Neches, 1839

Battle of the Nueces, 1862
Battle of Palmito Ranch, 1865
Battle of Palo Alto, 1846
Battle of Refugio, 1836
Battle of Resaca de la Palma, 1846
Battle of Rosillo, 1813
Battle of Sabine Pass, 1863
Battle of Salado, 1813, 1842
Battle of San Jacinto, 1835, 1836, 1869, 1891
Battle of San Patricio, 1836
Battle of Velasco, 1832
Battle of Val Verde, 1862, 1885
Battle of Village Creek, 1841
Battle on the San Gabriels, 1838
Battlegrounds, 1907
Battles, 1813, 1824, 1832, 1835, 1836, 1838, 1839, 1840, 1841, 1842, 1846, 1852, 1862, 1863, 1864, 1865, 1873
Bay View College, 1894
Bayland Orphans' Home Association, 1888, 1914
Bayland Orphans' Home for Boys, 1866, 1867, 1888, 1914
Baylor, Henry W., 1858
Baylor County, 1858
Baylor Belton, 1886
Baylor Female Academy, 1865, 1886
Baylor Female College, 1865, 1886
Baylor Hospital, 1903
Baylor University, 1845, 1846, 1854, 1886, 1887, 1900, 1909, 1918
Baylor University College of Dentistry, 1918
Baylor University College of Medicine, 1900
Beales' Rio Grande Colony, 1833, 1834
Beals, David T., 1877
Bean, Judge Roy, 1896
Bean Indians, 1683
Beau Monde, the Magazine of Fashion, 1895
Beaumont, Texas, 1886, 1901
Beaumont and Great Northern Railway Company, 1905
Beaumont and Saratoga Transportation Company, 1905
Beaumont, Sour Lake, and Port Arthur Traction Company, 1903

Beaumont, Sour Lake, and Western Railway Company, 1904
Beaumont Wharf and Terminal Company, 1899
Beaver Cave, 1896
Bee, Barnard E., 1857
Bee County, 1857, 1858
Beitonijure Indians, 1684
Belknap, William G., 1851
Belknap Rifles, 1884
Bell, Peter H., 1850
Bell County, 1850, 1865
Belo, Alfred H., 1878, 1885
Belton, Texas, 1886
Belton Academy, 1886
Benedictine Sisters, 1919
Benevolent and Protective Order of Elks, 1865
Bergman, Josef Ernst, 1849
Bernard, Port of, 1805
Bethel Baptist Church, 1841
Bettina Community, 1847
Bexar, Siege of, 1835
Bexar Archives, 1899
Bexar County, 1836, 1917
Bexar Manufacturing Company, 1850
Bexar Territory, 1862
Bibit Indians, 1675
Bidai Indians, 1749
Big Hill, Texas, 1867
Bilby, J.S., 1901
Bilingual Newspapers, 1823
Binford University, 1889
Bird's Creek Indian Fight, 1839
Bird's Fort, 1841, 1843
Bishop College, 1881, 1885
Black, William, 1851
Black Bean Episode, 1843
Black Colleges, 1900
Black Horse, 1876
Black Schools, 1905
Black's Fort, 1851
Blackwell, Enid, and Texas Railway Company, 1901
Blacks, 1865, 1869, 1917
Blair, C.C., 1860
Blair's Fort, 1860
Blanco County, 1858

126

Blanco Masonic High School, 1883, 1884

Blanco Masonic University, 1874, 1875, 1883

Blanco Public School, 1884

Blind Institute, 1905, 1915

Blinn, Christian, 1889

Blinn Memorial College, 1883, 1889

Bliss, William Wallace S., 1854

Blockades, 1836

Bluebonnets, 1901

Board to Calculate the Ad Valorem Tax Rate, 1907

Board of Control, 1914, 1919

Board of Medical Censors, 1837

Board of Water Engineers, 1913, 1916

Bobida Indians, 1684

Bobole Indians, 1665

Boggy Creek, 1840

Bohemian, 1898

Boll Weevil, 1892

Bollworm, Pink, 1916, 1917

Bonham, Texas, 1867, 1880, 1884, 1913

Books, 1857

Borden, Gail, Jr., 1876

Borden County, 1876, 1892

Boren, T.E., 1885

Borobama Indians, 1683

Borrado Indians, 1693

Bosque, Fernando del, 1675

Bosque County, 1850, 1853, 1854, 1860

Bosque Female Seminary and Male College, 1858

Bosque-Larios Expedition, 1675

Bosque River, 1854

Bosqueville Male and Female College, 1862

Boston, Texas, 1844, 1856

Boundaries, 1848, 1850, 1896, 1911

Boundary Disputes, 1806, 1836, 1850, 1871, 1884

Bowie, James, 1795, 1828, 1830, 1836, 1840

Bowie County, 1719, 1838, 1840, 1841, 1856, 1891

Bowles, Chief, 1839

Box, Michael James, 1861

Box Colony, 1861

Boyle, David, 1873

Brackett, Albert G., 1856

Brady, J.F., 1876

Brahman Cattle, 1895, 1919

Brands, Cattle, 1837, 1881, 1888

Brann, William C., 1891, 1894

Brazoria, Texas, 1832, 1834, 1837, 1838, 1839, 1845

Brazoria County, 1826, 1836, 1839, 1847

Brazos County, 1841, 1842, 1843

Brazos Courier, 1839

Brazos Eagle, 1868

Brazos Farmer, 1842

Brazos Flood, 1899

Brazos and Galveston Railroad Company, 1838

Brazos Indian Reservation, 1854, 1855, 1858, 1859

Brazos Institute, 1860

Brazos Largos Indians, 1794

Brazos Planter, 1845

Brazos River, 1687, 1707, 1732, 1821, 1830, 1835, 1836, 1842, 1850, 1899

Brazos River Missionary Baptist Association, 1860

Brenham, Texas, 1853, 1883, 1891, 1912

Brewster, Henry P., 1887

Brewster County, 1880, 1887, 1891

"Brick Academy", 1846

Bridges, 1858, 1909

Bright Star Educational Society, 1860

Briscoe, Andrew, 1835, 1876

Briscoe County, 1876, 1892

Britain, 1838

Brite Bible College, 1895

British-Texan Diplomacy, 1842

Britton, A.M., 1878

Broocks-Border-Wall Feud, 1900

Brooks, James Abijah, 1911

Brooks Air Force Base, 1917, 1918

Brooks County, 1911, 1912

Brown, Henry S., 1856

Brown, Jacob, 1846

Brown County, 1856, 1858, 1862

Brownsboro, Texas, 1845

Brownsville, Texas, 1846, 1855, 1858, 1859, 1864, 1865

Brownsville and Matamoros Bridge

Company, 1909
Brownsville Street and Interurban Railroad Company, 1912
Brownsville Wharf Case, 1871
Brownwood, Texas, 1889
Brownwood North and South Railway Company, 1910
Brutus, 1836
Bryan, Texas, 1868
Bryan Baptist Academy, 1909
Bryan and Central Texas Interurban, 1918
Bryan and College Interurban Railway Company, 1910
Buchanan, James, 1858
Buchanan County, 1858, 1861
Buchel, County, 1887, 1897
Buckeye Rangers, 1836
Buckner Orphans Home, 1879, 1880
Buffaloes, 1875
Buffalo Bayou, 1837
Buffalo Bayou, Brazos, and Colorado Railway, 1850, 1853
Buffalo Bayou Ship Channel, 1869
Buffalo Gap, Texas, 1885
Buffalo Gap College, 1883, 1885
Buffalo Hide Business, 1876
Buffalo Wallow Fight, 1874
Buildings, 1779, 1856
Bullis, John L., 1917
Bullock House, 1839
Bureau of Economic Geology, 1909
Bureau of Labor Statistics, 1909
Burkburnett, Texas, 1913, 1918
Burkburnett Oil Field, 1913, 1918
Burleson, Albert Sidney, 1913
Burleson, Edward, 1839, 1841, 1846
Burleson, Richard B., 1856
Burleson, Rufus C., 1895
Burleson College, 1895, 1899
Burleson County, 1830, 1842, 1846

Burleson Female Institute, 1856
Burnet, David G., 1836, 1838, 1841, 1852
Burnet, Texas, 1851
Burnet County, 1841, 1849, 1851, 1852, 1854
Burnett, Samuel Burk, 1867
Burnetta College, 1896

Burr's Ferry, 1863
Burr's Ferry, Browndell, and Chester Railroad, 1906
Business Firms, 1834, 1836, 1838, 1841, 1885, 1907, 1908, 1910, 1918, 1919
Butler, Anthony, 1834
Butler College, 1905
Butterfield Overland Mail Route, 1858
Byars' Institute, 1867

C

Caai Indians, 1691
Cabellos Blancos Indians, 1693
Cabeza de Vaca, Alvar Nuñez, 1528
Cabeza Indians, 1693
Cabia Indians, 1690
Cabra Indians, 1785
Cacaxtle Indians, 1665
Cachopostale Indians, 1785
Caddo Indians, 1542, 1836, 1843, 1854
Caddo Lake, 1910
Cagaya Indians, 1691
Caiasban Indians, 1691
Caimane Indians, 1683
Caisquetebana Indians, 1690
Caldwell, Mathew, 1848
Caldwell County, 1848
Calhoun, John C., 1846
Calhoun College 1880, 1887
Calhoun County, 1837, 1840, 1846
California, 1857
California Column, 1862
Call, Loren H., 1917
Call Field, 1917
Callahan, James Hughes, 1855, 1877
Callahan County, 1862, 1877
Callahan Expedition, 1855
Calvert, Waco, and Brazos Valley Railroad Company, 1899, 1901
Camama Indians, 1720
Camels, 1855, 1856, 1857
Cameron, Ewen, 1848
Cameron, Texas, 1848
Cameron County, 1846, 1848
Camino Real, 1691
Camp, John Lafayette, 1874
Camp Austin, 1848
Camp Belknap, 1862

Camp Ben McCulloch, 1896
Camp Breckenridge, 1862
Camp Bullis, 1917
Camp Casa Blanca, 1852
Camp Cazneau, 1840
Camp Charlotte, 1874
Camp Clark, 1861
Camp Collier, 1862
Camp Colorado, 1855, 1856, 1857, 1861
Camp Concordia, 1868
Camp Cooper, 1856, 1861
Camp Corpus Christi, 1850
Camp County, 1874
Camp Crawford, 1849, 1850
Camp Cureton, 1862
Camp Davis, 1862
Camp Dix, 1862
Camp Drum, 1852
Camp Eagle Pass, 1849
Camp Elizabeth, 1853
Camp Ford, 1864
Camp Funston, 1917
Camp Grierson, 1878
Camp Groce, 1862
Camp Harney, 1851
Camp Hatch, 1867, 1868
Camp Holland, 1918
Camp Hudson, 1857
Camp Independence, 1836, 1837
Camp Ives, 1859, 1860, 1861
Camp Joseph E. Johnston, 1852
Camp Kelly, 1868
Camp Kenny, 1874
Camp Liendo, 1865
Camp Llano, 1862
Camp Logan, 1917
Camp Mabry, 1890
Camp MacArthur, 1917
Camp McMillan, 1862
Camp Merrill, 1852
Camp Montel, 1862, 1870
Camp Nelson, 1862
Camp Nowlin, 1859
Camp Nueces, 1862
Camp Pecan, 1862
Camp Rabb, 1862
Camp Radziminski, 1858
Camp Sabinal, 1856
Camp Salmon, 1862

Camp San Elizaro, 1849
Camp San Felipe, 1857
Camp on the San Pedro, 1857
Camp San Saba, 1852, 1862
Camp Stanley, 1917
Camp Travis, 1917
Camp Van Camp, 1859
Camp Verde, 1855, 1856, 1862
Camp Wichita, 1870
Camp Wood, 1857, 1861
Campbell, H.H., 1878
Campbell, Texas, 1892, 1903
Cana Indians, 1720
Canaan, Texas, 1876
Canabatinu Indians, 1691
Canadian, Texas, 1886, 1888, 1904
Canadian Academy, 1904, 1912
Canadian River, 900, 1719, 1877
Canales, Antonio, 1842
Canals, 1850, 1913
Canaq Indians, 1693
Canary Islanders, 1731
Canary Islands, 1722
Canby, Edward R.S., 1865
Cancepne Indians, 1748
Candalaria, Señora Andrea Castanon, 1891
Cane Belt Railroad Company, 1893
Cannaha Indians, 1687
Cannahio Indians, 1687
Cannon, 1836
Canonediba Indians, 1691
Canonizochitoui Indians, 1691
Cantey Indians, 1687
Cantona Indians, 1771
Canu Indians, 1691
Canyon, Texas, 1910
Capers, William Theodotus, 1914
Capitals of Texas, 1721, 1772, 1833, 1836, 1837, 1840, 1842, 1845
Capitol Freehold Land and Investment Company, Limited, 1882, 1885
Capitol of Texas, 1881, 1882, 1888
Caquixadaquix Indians, 1691
Car-Stable Convention, 1892
Carballedo y Zuñiga, Andrés G. Barcia, 1723
Carhart, Lewis Henry, 1879
Carleton, James H., 1862

129

RANCH HANDS at the Matador Ranch in 1883. The ranch was started in 1878 and was purchased by the Matador Land and Cattle Company in 1882.

— *Photo from the Southwest Collection, Texas Tech University.*
Copy from The University of Texas Institute of Texan Cultures.

Carlisle Military Academy, 1890
Carlsbad, Texas, 1910, 1912
Carlton College, 1865, 1867, 1887, 1913
Caro Northern Railway Company, 1894
Carpenter's Union, 1860
Carpetbag Era, 1867
Carr, Mattie F., 1894
Carr-Burdette College, 1894, 1913
Carrizo Indians, 1768, 1855, 1886
Carroll, Benjamin H., Jr., 1912, 1914
Carson, Samuel Price, 1836, 1876
Carson County, 1876
Cart War, 1857
Carthage, Texas, 1885, 1890
Carvajal, José Luis, 1830
Carvajal Crossing, 1830
Casañas de Jesús María, Francisco, 1690
Casas, Juan Bautista de las, 1811
Casas Moradas Indians, 1693
Casas Revolution, 1811
Case School, 1866
Casiba Indians, 1691
Casino Club, 1857, 1858
Caso Indians, 1748
Cass, Lewis, 1846
Cass County, 1846, 1850, 1856, 1861, 1871
Cassia Indians, 1687
Castañeda, Francisco, 1835
Castaño de Sosa, Gaspar, 1590
Castillo, Diego del, 1650
Castillo Maldonado, Alonso de, 1528
Castro, Henri, 1842, 1876
Castro County, 1876, 1891
Castroville, Texas, 1920
Cat Spring, 1849
Catholics, 1852, 1881, 1885, 1894, 1907
Catqueza Indians, 1691
Cattle Brands, 1844, 1872, 1881, 1898
Cattle Breeding, 1919
Cattle Companies, 1880, 1882, 1884
Cattle Drives, 1915
Cattle in Texas, 1690, 1876, 1880, 1883
Cattle Trails, 1866, 1883
The Cattleman, 1914
Cattlemen's Organizations, 1877
Caula Indians, 1684

Caux Indians, 1719
Cava Indians, 1740
Caves, 1896, 1900
Caverns, 1896, 1900
Caverns of Sonora, 1900
Caxo Indians, 1691
Caynaaya Indians, 1691
Cazneau, William Leslie, 1853
Cedar Valley Lands and Cattle Company, 1885
Celebrations, 1891
Cenizo Indians, 1698
Centennial, Texas, 1876
Centennial Masonic Institute, 1876
Central College 1886, 1894
Central Male and Female Institute, 1850
Central and Montgomery Railway, 1877
Central National Road of the Republic of Texas, 1844
Central Nazarene College, 1909, 1911
Central Plains Academy, 1890
Central Plains College and Conservatory of Music, 1907, 1910
Central Texas and Northwestern Railroad Company, 1881
Chadbourne, Theodore L., 1852
Chambers, Thomas Jefferson, 1834, 1858, 1861, 1863
Chambers of Commerce, 1840, 1845, 1906, 1908, 1910, 1918, 1919
Chambers County, 1858, 1867, 1891, 1918
Chambers Terraqueous Transportation Company, 1854
Chapel Hill College, 1850
Chappell Hill, Texas, 1855
Chappell Hill College, 1850, 1852
Chappell Hill Male and Female Institute, 1852
Chaquantu Indians, 1700
Charitable Institutions, 1887, 1908
Charnwood Institute, 1865, 1869
Chayopine Indians, 1750
Chenti Indians, 1732
Cherokee, Texas, 1895
Cherokee Academy, 1848, 1893
Cherokee Baptist Association, 1853
Cherokee County, 1687, 1835, 1846,

131

1847, 1894

Cherokee Indians, 1836, 1837, 1839, 1846

Cherokee Junior College, 1911

Cherokee War, 1839

Chicago, Rock Island, and Gulf Railway Company, 1893, 1902, 1903

Chicago, Rock Island, and Mexico Railway Company, 1900

Chicago, Rock Island, and Texas Railway Company, 1892

Chicago, Texas, and Mexican Central Railway, 1879

"Chicken Salad Case", 1915

Chihuahua Trail, 1839

Childress, George C., 1876

Childress County, 1876, 1880, 1887

Chinese in Texas, 1870

Chisholm Trail, 1857, 1867

Choctaw, Oklahoma, and Texas Railroad Company, 1901

Choctaw Tom, 1858

Christ Church, Matagorda, 1839

Christian Church (Disciples of Christ), 1841, 1860, 1913

The Christian Courier, 1888

Christian Messenger, 1880

Christian Preacher, 1880

Christian Science Church, 1889

Church of Christ, 1880, 1884, 1894, 1903, 1904, 1906, 1907, 1909

Church Hill Academy, 1853, 1854

Church of the Nazarene, 1898, 1908

Church Publications, 1847, 1849

Churches, 1841, 1860, 1889, 1898, 1905, 1906, 1914

Cibolo Creek, 1830

Cincinnati, Ohio, 1836

Cisco and Northeastern Railway Company, 1918

The Citizen, 1843

Citizen's White Primary, 1898

Civil Disturbance, 1859

Civilian, 1838

Clarendon, Texas, 1898

Clarendon College and University Training School, 1898

Clarendon *News,* 1879

Clark, Edward, 1861

Clark, John B., 1852

Clark, Thomas Marshall, 1894

Clark, William T., 1872

Clark Seminary, 1872

Clarksville, Texas, 1840, 1841, 1842, 1847, 1848

Clarksville Academy, 1842

Clarksville Female Academy, 1840

Clarksville Female Institute, 1848, 1854

Clarksville Male Academy, 1847

Clarksville Male and Female Academy, 1847, 1854

Clay, Henry, 1857

Clay County, 1857, 1861, 1873

Clebarro College, 1909

Cleburne, Texas, 1909

Cleburne Male and Female Institute, 1866

Cleveland College, 1884, 1889

Clifton Academy, 1860, 1896

Clubs, 1865, 1891, 1898, 1899

Coahuila, 1833

Coahuila Manufacturing Company, 1830

Coahuila and Texas, State of, 1824, 1827, 1833, 1834

Coal, 1884, 1888, 1917

Coal Companies, 1888, 1917

Coapite Indians, 1722

Coaque Indians, 1528

Coat of Arms, 1839

Cochran, Robert, 1876

Cochran County, 1876, 1901

Cocoma Indians, 1675

Cody, A.J., 1841

Coffee, Holland, 1845

Coke, Richard, 1889

Coke County, 1852, 1889

Colabrote Indians, 1684

Colas Largas Indians, 1693

Cold Springs Female College, 1853

Coleman, R.M., 1858

Coleman County, 1856, 1858, 1862, 1876

College Hill Institute, 1884

College of Marshall, 1912, 1917

College of Mines and Metallurgy, 1919

Colleges, 1837, 1839-1861, 1863-1867, 1869-1873, 1875-1920

1875, 1881

Corsicana, Texas, 1887, 1889, 1898, 1899

Corsicana Female Literary Institute, 1870

Corsicana Masonic Lodge, 1870

Corsicana Oil Field, 1895

Corsicana Petroleum Company, 1899

Cortina, Juan Nepomuceno, 1859

Cortina War, 1859

Coryell, James, 1854

Coryell County, 1854, 1916

Cós, Martín Perfecto de, 1835

Cotoname Indians, 1886

Cottle, George W., 1876

Cottle County, 1876, 1892

Cotton, 1846

Cotton Jammer's Association, 1879

Cotton Mills, 1830

Cotton Palace, 1894

Council House Fight, 1840

Counties, 1836-1843, 1846, 1848-1858, 1860-1862, 1864, 1866, 1868-1871, 1873-1893, 1896, 1897, 1899, 1901-1905, 1907, 1908, 1910-1913, 1917

Courtney Male and Female School, 1869

Courtland, Alabama, 1835

Court Decisions, 1867, 1869

Cowboy Strike, 1883

Cowboys, 1883

Cowden Ranch, 1881

Cox, Paris, 1879

Coxey's Army, 1894

Crane, M.M., 1897

Crane, William Carey, 1887

Crane County, 1887

Crawford, George W., 1849

Crawford, W.C., 1839

Crazy Well, 1885

Creameries, 1885

Croaker, 1842

Crockett, David, 1786, 1875, 1897

Crockett, Texas, 1886

Crockett County, 1855, 1875, 1891

Croghan, George, 1849

Crosby, Stephen, 1886

Crosby County, 1879, 1880, 1884, 1886, 1890

Crosbyton-South Plains Railroad, 1910, 1915

Cruiamo Indians, 1693

Crystal City and Uvalde Railroad Company, 1909, 1912

Cuba, 1898

Cuero, Texas, 1912

Cujaco Indians, 1684

Cujalo Indians, 1684

Cujane Indians, 1722

Culberson, Charles A., 1894, 1898

Culberson, David B., 1911

Culberson County, 1750, 1911, 1912

Cullinan, Joseph Stephen, 1898, 1901

Cumberland Presbyterian Church, 1829, 1837, 1843, 1849, 1850, 1883, 1890

Cummings, James, 1826

Cummings, John, 1826

Cummings, William, 1826

Cunquebaco Indians, 1684

Curry-Comb Ranch, 1880

Curtain Club, 1909

Custer, George A., 1865

Customhouses, 1838

Czechs, 1849

Czech Newspapers, 1879

Czech Language, 1885

D

Daily Advertiser, 1841

Daily Bulletin, 1841

Daily Courier, 1840

Daily Globe, 1845

Daily Texan, 1900, 1913

Daily Texian, 1841

Daily Times, 1840, 1857

Daingerfield, Texas, 1852, 1856

Dairying, 1880

Dallam, James M., 1846, 1876

Dallam County, 1876, 1882, 1891

Dallas, George M., 1846

Dallas, Texas, 1841, 1854, 1856, 1859, 1873, 1875-1877, 1879, 1880, 1885-1889, 1895, 1900, 1905, 1909, 1910, 1912-1915, 1917-1920

Dallas Art Association, 1903

Dallas and Cleburne Railroad, 1876

Dallas, Cleburne, and Southwestern Railway Company, 1902
Dallas College, 1878
Dallas County, 1846, 1869, 1885, 1911
Dallas *Daily Herald,* 1874
Dallas *Evening Herald,* 1886, 1888
Dallas *Evening Times,* 1876, 1888
Dallas Fair and Exposition, 1886
Dallas Free Public Art Gallery, 1909
Dallas and Greenville Railway, 1886
Dallas *Herald,* 1873
Dallas *Journal,* 1914
Dallas Little Theatre, 1920
Dallas Male and Female College, 1869, 1870
Dallas *Morning News,* 1885, 1914
Dallas Museum of Fine Arts, 1909
Dallas, Palestine, and Southeast Railroad, 1878
Dallas Terminal Railway and Union Depot Company, 1884
Dallas *Times-Herald,* 1888
Dallas and Waco Railway Company, 1886
Dallas *Weekly Herald,* 1873
Dallas and Wichita Railway Company, 1871
Dams, 1901, 1911, 1918, 1920
Danes in Texas, 1850
Daniel Baker College, 1889
Daquio Indians, 1687
Datana Indians, 1691
Datcho Indians, 1687
Daughters of the American Revolution, Texas Society of, 1899
Daughters of the Republic of Texas, 1891, 1905
Davenport, Iowa, 1884
Davilla Institute, 1872
Davis, Edmund J., 1869, 1871
Davis, Jefferson, 1854, 1861, 1875, 1887
Davis County, 1861, 1871
Dawson, Nicholas M., 1876
Dawson County, 1858, 1876, 1905
Dawson Massacre, 1842
Day Land and Cattle Company, 1884
Dayton-Goose Creek Railroad, 1917
Deadose Indians, 1721, 1751
Deaf, Dumb, and Blind Institute for

Colored Youth, 1887
Deaf Institute, 1856
Deaf Smith County, 1876, 1890
Debating and Declamation League of Texas Schools, 1911
Debating League of Texas High Schools, 1910, 1911
Decatur, Texas, 1891
Decatur Baptist College, 1891, 1897
De Chene's Hotel, 1844
Declaration of Independence, 1836
Declaration of November 7, 1835, 1835
Decrees, 1829
Defense Efforts, 1916, 1917
De Kalb and Red River Railroad Company, 1891
Delaware Indians, 1820
De León, Alonso, 1690
De León, Martín, 1824
De León's Colony, 1824
Della Plain Male and Female Institute, 1890
Delores Settlement, 1834
Del Rio, Texas, 1857, 1884, 1889
Del Rio *Dot,* 1884
Delta County, 1870
De Mézières, Anthanase, 1779
Democratic State Convention, 1892
Democrats, 1873, 1892
De Morse, Charles, 1842
Denison, Bonham, and New Orleans Railway Company, 1887
Denison and Pacific Railway Company, 1878, 1880
Denison and Pacific Suburban Railway Company, 1895
Denison and Southeast Railway Company, 1877, 1880
Denison and Washita Valley Railroad Company, 1886
Denton, John B., 1846
Denton, Texas, 1868, 1890, 1900, 1903, 1904, 1909
Denton County, 1846, 1887
Denton *Monitor,* 1868
Department of Agriculture, 1907
Department of Bexar, 1836
Department of Public Health, 1903
Department of Insurance, Statistics, and History, 1876

Department of Louisiana and Texas, 1865
De Solis, Gaspar José, 1767, 1768
De Soto, Hernando, 1542
Detobiti Indians, 1684
DeWitt, Green C., 1825, 1846
DeWitt County, 1842, 1846, 1865
DeWitt's Colony, 1825
De Zavala, Lorenzo, 1858
Diaz, Porfirio, 1891
Dickens, J., 1876
Dickens County, 1876, 1891
Dickson Colored Orphanage, 1900, 1901
Dico Indians, 1691
Die Freie Presse fuer Texas, 1865
Dientes Alazanes Indians, 1693
Diju Indians, 1684
Dimmit, Philip, 1858
Dimmit County, 1858, 1880
Diplomacy, 1836, 1841, 1842, 1853, 1914
Disciples of Christ, 1841, 1851, 1860, 1878, 1880, 1888, 1893, 1894, 1896, 1905, 1906, 1909, 1910, 1913
Disease Control, 1903
Division of Texas, 1850, 1852, 1866, 1870, 1871, 1906
Documents, 1850
Dodge City, Kansas, 1876
Doguene Indians, 1528
Dolores Mission, 1716
Dominican Republic, 1853
Dominican Sisters, 1882
Donelson, Andrew Jackson, 1844
Donley, Stockton P., 1882
Donley County, 1882
Douay, Anastasius, 1687
Draymen, 1880
Dripping Springs Academy, 1881
Duels, 1837
Durham Cattle, 1848
Duval, John C., 1858
Duval, Thomas H., 1858
Duval County, 1858, 1876, 1891
Dyer, Leigh, 1877

E

Eagle Island Plantation, 1826
Eagle Lake, 1900
Eagle Pass, Texas, 1675, 1698, 1699, 1706, 1707, 1708, 1754, 1849
Early-Hasley Feud, 1865, 1869
East Line and Red River Railroad Company, 1871, 1881, 1893
East Texas Baptist Association, 1905
East Texas Baptist College, 1912
East Texas Baptist Institute, 1894, 1895, 1920
East Texas and Gulf Railway, 1917
East Texas Normal College, 1890, 1895, 1917
East Texas Railroad Company, 1880
Eastern Texas Female College, 1854, 1865
Eastern Texas Railroad, 1852, 1900
Eastland, William M., 1858
Eastland County, 1858, 1860, 1862, 1864, 1873
Eastland, Wichita Falls, and Gulf Railroad Company, 1919
Eastman, H.N., 1894
Eastman, H.P., 1894
Eastman College, 1894
Ebahamo Indians, 1690
Echancote Indians, 1684
Economic Geology, Bureau of, 1909
Ector, Mathew Duncan, 1887
Ector County, 1887, 1891
Ector's Brigade, 1862
Education, 1895, 1896, 1901, 1903
Educational Publications, 1883, 1887, 1914
Edwards, Haden, 1825, 1836, 1858
Edwards County, 1675, 1762, 1825, 1858, 1883
Edwards Plateau, 1690
Eight-Section Act, 1905
Eighteenth Amendment, 1918
Eighth Texas Infantry Battalion, 1862
El Cañon Mission, 1762
Election Laws, 1905
Elections, 1846, 1851, 1853, 1855,

1861, 1863, 1865, 1866, 1869, 1872, 1876, 1878, 1892, 1894, 1889, 1910, 1914, 1916

Electra Oil Field, 1911

Electric Fence, 1888

Elisabet Ney Museum, 1892, 1909

Eliza Russell, 1837

Elks Lodge, 1865

Ellington Air Force Base, 1917

Ellington Field, 1917

Eliot, Claude, 1842

Elliott, Joel H., 1875

Ellis, Richard, 1849

Ellis County, 1849, 1892

Ellison Springs Indian Fight, 1864

Elm Creek, 1918

El Mejicano, 1813

Elmwood Institute, 1898

El Paso, Texas, 1584, 1659, 1675, 1680, 1682, 1683, 1849, 1856, 1857, 1870, 1877, 1885, 1894, 1896, 1914, 1919

El Paso County, 1849, 1850

El Paso and Northeastern Railroad Company, 1896

El Paso Southern Railway Company, 1897

El Paso Southwestern Railroad Company, 1902

El Paso Terminal Railroad Company, 1901

El Señor San José, 1715

Ellwood, Isaac L., 1891

Emancipation, 1865

Emerson College, 1903

Emet Indians, 1689, 1690, 1750

Emory, Texas, 1902

Encinal County, 1856, 1899

English Universal Immigration Company, 1850

Episcopal Church, 1852, 1860, 1878, 1889

Epperson, B.H., 1851

Equal Suffrage League, 1903

Erath, George B., 1856

Erie Telegraph and Telephone Company, 1883

Erigoanna Indians, 1687

Ervipiame Indians, 1675, 1707, 1716, 1732

Escanjaque Indians, 1650

Espejo, Antonio de, 1583

Espinosa, Isidro Felix de, 1708

Espíritu Santo de Zuñiga Mission, 1722

Espopolame Indians, 1675

Esquien Indians, 1750

Estacado, Texas, 1890

Estacado and Gulf Railroad Company, 1908

Estepisa Indians, 1750

Europeans in Texas, 1842

Evangelical Lutheran College, 1870, 1891, 1912

Evening Herald, 1886

Evening Journal, 1885

Evergreen Plantation, 1847

Ewell, Richard Stoddert, 1852

Ewing College, 1860

Expeditions, 1528, 1540, 1542, 1581, 1650, 1654, 1682, 1685, 1690, 1740, 1806, 1812, 1819, 1832, 1841, 1842, 1843, 1877, 1896

Experiment Stations, 1914

Eyerly, T.L., 1907

"Eyes of Texas," 1903, 1906

F

Fairfield, Texas, 1869, 1872

Fairfield Female Academy, 1858, 1859, 1860

Fairview, Texas, 1879

Fairs and Expositions, 1859, 1862, 1886, 1894

Falls County, 1835, 1839, 1850

Fannin, James W., Jr., 1836, 1837

Fannin County, 1837, 1838, 1867, 1876

Fannin Battleground State Historic Site, 1914

Fannin Farmers' Review, 1884

Far West, 1847

Farm Implements, 1843

Farm Organizations, 1873, 1875, 1876, 1878, 1879, 1887, 1890, 1902, 1906, 1911, 1912, 1920

Farmers' Alliance, 1875, 1879, 1886, 1887

Farmers' Alliance and Co-operative Union of America, 1887

137

Farmers' Bank, 1911
Farmers' Educational and Co-operative Union of America, 1902
Farmers' Home Improvement Society, 1890, 1906, 1911
Farmers' Improvement Agricultural College, 1906
Farmers' Union, 1887, 1902
Favor, Milton, 1852
Fayette County, 1837, 1838, 1843
Fayetteville, Texas, 1849, 1860
Fayetteville Academy, 1849, 1860
Fayetteville Male and Female Academy, 1860
Federal Reserve Bank, 1914
Fence Cutting, 1884
Fences, 1888
Ferguson, James E., 1914-1917
Ferguson Forum, 1917
Ferries, 1821, 1830, 1836, 1838, 1846, 1863
Ferris, Texas, 1892
Ferris Institute, 1892
Festivals, 1912
Feuds, 1839, 1844, 1865, 1867, 1869, 1873, 1875, 1877, 1888, 1889, 1894, 1900
Fiesta de San Jacinto, 1891
Fifty Cent Act, 1879, 1883
Fine Arts, 1911
Firm Foundation, 1884
First National Bank of Galveston, 1865
First United States Cavalry Volunteers, 1898
Fisher, Samuel Rhoads, 1876
Fisher, William S., 1842
Fisher County, 1876, 1886
Fisher-Miller Land Grant, 1842
Fitzsimmons-Maher Heavyweight Fight, 1896
Flags of Texas, 1836, 1839
The Flash, 1836
Flechas Chiquitos Indians, 1684
Flechas Feas Indians, 1683
Fleming, Margaret, 1874
Floods, 1899
Floyd, Delphin Ward, 1876
Floyd County, 1876, 1890
Foard, Robert, 1891

Foard County, 1891
Foley County, 1887, 1897
Folklore, 1909, 1910
Food Processing, 1900, 1910
Foote, Henry Stuart, 1850
Ford, John S., 1852, 1864
Ford and Neighbors Trail, 1849
Foreign Language Newspapers, 1853, 1885
Foreigners in Texas, 1821, 1825, 1849, 1850, 1854, 1870, 1885, 1907
Forest Hill Plantation, 1847
Forests, 1914
Forshey, Caleb G., 1854
Forsyth, A., 1880
Forsyth, J., 1880
Fort Anahuac, 1831
Fort Belknap, 1851, 1858
Fort Bend, 1821, 1837
Fort Bend County, 1830, 1837, 1888, 1899
Fort Bliss, 1848, 1854, 1868
Fort Boggy, 1840
Fort Brown, 1846
Fort Burleson, 1839
Fort Chadbourne, 1852
Fort Cienaga, 1852
Fort Clark, 1857, 1862
Fort Colorado, 1836
Fort Concho, 1853, 1867, 1868
Fort Crawford, 1839
Fort Crockett, 1897
Fort Croghan, 1849
Fort Davis, 1854, 1862
Fort Defiance, 1836
Fort Duncan, 1849
Fort Elliott, 1875
Fort Esperanza, 1863
Fort Ewell, 1852
Fort Fisher, 1837
Fort Fitzhugh, 1847
Fort Gates, 1849
Fort Graham, 1849
Fort Griffin, 1867
Fort Griffin *Echo*, 1879, 1883
Fort Hancock, 1882
Fort Houston, 1835
Fort Hudson, 1857
Fort Inge, 1849
Fort Inglish, 1837

Fort Jackson, 1866
Fort Johnson, 1840
Fort Lancaster, 1855
Fort Leaton, 1846
Fort Lincoln, 1849
Fort Lipantitlán, 1835
Fort McIntosh, 1849, 1850
Fort McKavett, 1852
Fort Marcy, 1845
Fort Martin Scott, 1848
Fort Mason, 1851, 1858
Fort Merrill, 1850
Fort Milam, 1835
Fort Moritas, 1852
Fort Parker, 1834, 1836
Fort Pena Colorado, 1880
Fort Phantom Hill, 1851
Fort Pickettville, 1854
Fort Polk, 1846
Fort Quitman, 1858
Fort Ramirez, 1920
Fort Richardson, 1867, 1871
Fort Riley, 1852
Fort Ringgold, 1848
Fort Sabine, 1865
Fort St. Louis, 1685
Fort Sam Houston, 1879
Fort San Jacinto, 1835, 1898
Fort Sherman, 1838
Fort Sill Reservation, 1876
Fort Smith, 1846
Fort Stockton, 1859
Fort Stockton, Texas, 1894
Fort Sullivan, 1835
Fort Tenoxtitlán, 1830
Fort Terán, 1831
Fort Terrett, 1852
Fort Travis, 1836
Fort Worth, 1849, 1898
Fort Worth, Texas, 1848, 1885, 1890, 1896, 1901, 1910, 1911, 1914
Fort Worth Belt Railway Company, 1895
Fort Worth and Denver Terminal Railway Company, 1890
Fort Worth and New Orleans Terminal Railway Company, 1885
Fort Worth and Rio Grande Railway Company, 1887
Fort Worth *Star-Telegram*, 1879, 1906

Fort Worth University, 1881, 1889
Forts, 1685, 1821, 1828, 1830, 1831, 1834, 1835-1840, 1845-1852, 1854, 1855, 1857-1859, 1863, 1865-1868, 1875, 1879, 1880, 1882, 1897, 1898, 1920
Fountain, Albert J., 1896
Four-Section Act, 1895
Four Sixes Ranch, 1867, 1874, 1900
Fourth United States Cavalry, 1871
Fowler Institute, 1850
"Fowler's Folly," 1918
France, 1839-1842, 1848, 1917
Franco-Texan Land Company, 1876
Franco-Texian Bill, 1841
Franklin, Benjamin C., 1875
Franklin College, 1856
Franklin County, 1875
Fraternal Organizations, 1828, 1835, 1861, 1865, 1872
Frazier, Bud, 1894
Fredericksburg, Texas, 1847, 1848
Fredericksburg College, 1876
Fredericksburg and Northern Railway Company, 1917
Fredonian Rebellion, 1826
Free State of Van Zandt, 1848
Freedmen's Bureau, 1865
Freeman, Thomas, 1806
Freeman's Red River Expedition, 1806
Freemasonry, 1828, 1835
Freestone County, 1850, 1851, 1858, 1860
Freestone County School Association, 1858
French Colonization in Texas, 1841, 1848, 1854, 1855
French Legation, 1841
Friends of Texas, 1836
Frio County, 1858, 1871
Frio River, 1690, 1858
Frisco System, 1881
Frontier Battalion, 1874
Frontier Defense, 1838, 1840, 1841, 1851, 1861, 1874
Frontier Echo, 1875, 1879
Frontier Regiment, 1861, 1862, 1874
Frying Pan Ranch, 1881

139

140

Gilmer Female College, 1854, 1856, 1860

Gincape Indians, 1785

Glasscock, George W., 1887

Glasscock County, 1887

Glen Eden Plantation, 1845

Glen Rose Collegiate Institute, 1889

Glen Rose, Texas, 1877

Glenblythe Plantation, 1859

Godwin, J.S., 1881

Goliad, Texas, 1749, 1754, 1794, 1835, 1836, 1848, 1852, 1902, 1914

Goliad Campaign, 1836

Goliad College, 1852

Goliad County, 1836, 1837, 1914

Goliad Declaration of Independence, 1835

Goliad Massacre, 1836

Gonzales, Rafael, 1836

Gonzales, Texas, 1835, 1841, 1852

Gonzales Branch Railroad Company, 1881

Gonzales College, 1852, 1853

Gonzales County, 1836, 1837, 1867

Goodnight, Charles, 1876, 1883, 1898

Goodnight Academy, 1898

Goodnight-Loving Trail, 1866

Goodnight Ranch, 1875

Goose Creek Oil Field, 1916

Goras, Juan Leal, 1731

Gorman, Mrs. Henrie C.L., 1898

Government Hospitals, 1920

Governors, 1767, 1779, 1805, 1811, 1851, 1853, 1855, 1865, 1869, 1878, 1894, 1910, 1914, 1916, 1917

Governor's Mansion, 1855

Graham, William M., 1849

Graham, Texas, 1854, 1871, 1877

Granbury College, 1873, 1889

Granbury's Texas Brigade, 1863

Grand Saline, Texas, 1920

Grange, 1873

Granger, Gordon, 1865

Granger, Georgetown, Austin, and San Antonio Railway Company, 1902

Granite Mountain and Marble Falls City Railroad, 1889

Grapefruit, 1904

Grass Fight, 1835

Gray, Peter W., 1876

Gray County, 1876, 1902

Grayson, Peter W., 1846

Grayson College, 1885, 1887

Grayson County, 1840, 1845, 1846, 1867, 1876, 1903, 1909

Great Galveston Storm, 1900

Great Hanging at Gainesville, 1862

Green, Thomas Jefferson, 1835, 1874

Green Mask Players, 1919

Greenback Movement, 1876, 1878

Greenville, Texas, 1895, 1899

Greenville and Northern Railway Company, 1914

Greenville and Whitewright Northern Traction Company, 1912, 1914

Greer County, 1860, 1866, 1873, 1896

Gregg, John, 1873

Gregg County, 1873

Gregory, Thomas Watt, 1914

Grenada, Mississippi, 1862

Gresham, Newt, 1902

Griffin, Charles, 1867

Grimes, Jesse, 1846

Grimes County, 1833, 1846, 1852, 1869

Groce's Retreat, 1833

Groveton, Lufkin, and Northern Railway Company, 1908

Grubbs Vocational College, 1917

Guacali Indians, 1693

Guadalajara, Diego de, 1654

Guadalupe College, 1841, 1848

Guadalupe Colored College, 1884

Guadalupe County, 1842, 1846, 1861, 1917

Guadalupe High School Association, 1849, 1855

Guadalupe Male and Female Academy, 1855

Guadalupe River, 1689, 1690, 1835

Guadalupe City, Texas, 1848

Guagejohe Indians, 1857

Guasa Indians, 1691

Gueiquesale Indians, 1675

Guerrero, Vicente, 1829

Guerrero Decree, 1829

Guisole Indians, 1864

Gulf, Beaumont, and Great Northern

Railway Company, 1898
Gulf, Beaumont, and Kansas City Railway Company, 1893
Gulf, Colorado, and Santa Fe Railway Company, 1873
Gulf and Interstate Railway Company, 1894
Gulf Intracoastal Waterway, 1913
Gulf and Northern Railroad Company, 1917
Gulf Oil Corporation, 1907
Gulf, Texas, and Western Railroad Company, 1908
Gumpusa Indians, 1794
Gun Factories, 1863
Gunter Bible College, 1903
Gunter v. *Texas Land and Mortgage Company,* 1891
Guitérrez-Magee Expedition, 1812, 1813

H

Hacanac Indian Province, 1542
Hacanac Indians, 1542
Hainai Indians, 1854
Hale, John C., 1876
Hale County, 1876, 1888
Hale Institute, 1859
Hall, Warren D.C., 1876
Hall County, 1876, 1890
Hallville Masonic Institute, 1873
Halsell, Glen, 1889
Halsell, W.E., 1889
Hamilton, Andrew Jackson, 1865
Hamilton, James, 1839, 1840, 1858
Hamilton, Robert, 1835
Hamilton County, 1842, 1858
Hamlin, Texas, 1909, 1911
Han Indians, 1528
Hanasine Indians, 1684
Hancock, Winfield Scott, 1882
Hand, C.T., 1865
Hangings, 1862
Hansford, John M., 1876
Hansford County, 1876, 1889
Hape Indians, 1675
Haqui Indians, 1687
Hardeman, Bailey, 1858

Hardeman, Thomas Jones, 1858
Hardeman County, 1858, 1876, 1884
Hardin, Augustine Blackburn, 1858
Hardin, Benjamin W., 1858
Hardin, Franklin, 1858
Hardin, Milton A., 1858
Hardin William, 1858
Hardin County, 1858
Hardin-Simmons University, 1891, 1892
Harris, Eli, 1819
Harris, John Richardson, 1837
Harris County, 1837, 1839, 1905
Harrisburg, Texas, 1835, 1852
Harrisburg and Brazos Railroad, 1841
Harrisburg County, 1836, 1837, 1839
Harrison, Jonas, 1839
Harrison County, 1839, 1841, 1873
Harrison Times, 1844
Hartley, Oliver C., 1876
Hartley, Rufus K., 1876
Hartley County, 1876, 1891
Hashknife Brand, 1872, 1881
Hashknife Ranch, 1872
Haskell, Charles, 1858
Haskell County, 1858, 1876, 1885
Hatch, John P., 1867
Hawkins, Texas, 1913
Hay Production, 1912
Hays, John Coffee, 1848
Hays County, 1848, 1852, 1896
Health Seekers, 1897
Hearne and Brazos Railway Company, 1891
Hebbronville, Texas, 1875
Hedgcoxe War, 1852
Hemphill, Texas, 1875, 1876
Hempstead, Texas, 1862
Henderson, James Pinckney, 1846
Henderson, Texas, 1845, 1849, 1850, 1864
Henderson County, 1845, 1846, 1873, 1885
Henderson Female College, 1849, 1856
Henderson Male and Female College, 1871
Henderson Masonic Female Institute, 1864, 1866
Henderson and Overton Branch

Railroad Company, 1874
Heniocane Indians, 1675
Henry, O., 1894
Henry College, 1892
Hereford, Texas, 1902
Hereford Cattle, 1876, 1883
Hereford College, 1908
Hereford College and Industrial
    School, 1902, 1905, 1908
Hermann's University, 1844, 1871
Herrera, Simón de, 1806, 1811
Hersey, Tim F., 1867
Hexagon House Hotel, 1897
Hiabu Indians, 1696
Hianagouy Indians, 1687
Hiantatsi Indians, 1687
Hidalgo y Costilla, Miguel, 1852
Hidalgo County, 1757, 1852, 1884
Highland Park, Texas, 1896
Highways, 1917
Hill, George W., 1853
Hill, Robert Thomas, 1887
Hill County, 1846, 1853
Hillsboro, Texas, 1849
Hillyer Female College, 1848
Hinehi Indians, 1684
Hinsa Indians, 1684
Historical Organizations, 1871, 1894,
    1897, 1909
Historical Publications, 1897, 1912
Hobby, Alfred Marmaduke, 1862
Hobby, W.P., 1918
Hockaday, Ela, 1913
Hockaday School, 1913, 1919
Hockley, George W., 1876
Hockley County, 1876, 1901
Hogg, James Stephen, 1851, 1891,
    1913
Holding Institute, 1880, 1891
Holiness Church, 1907, 1908, 1910
Holland, 1840
Holland's Magazine, 1876, 1903
Holy Cross Sisters, 1870
Homestead Laws, 1839, 1845
Honey Grove, Texas, 1888
Hood, John Bell, 1862, 1866
Hood County, 1866, 1873
"Hoodoo War," 1875
Hood's Texas Brigade, 1862

Hopewell Institute, 1867
Hopkins County, 1860
Horrell-Higgins Feud, 1873
Horse Marines, 1836
Hospitals, 1904, 1912, 1913, 1920
Hotels, 1836, 1839, 1844, 1847, 1859,
    1897
House, E.M., 1902
House of Barr and Davenport, 1798
Houston, Sam, 1793, 1835-1839,
    1842-1844, 1846, 1861, 1879
Houston, Texas, 1837-1841, 1843,
    1844, 1846, 1860, 1861, 1865, 1867,
    1869, 1872, 1873, 1876, 1880, 1882,
    1883, 1900, 1903, 1905, 1908, 1909,
    1912, 1917, 1919
Houston Academy, 1844, 1856
Houston and Austin Turnpike Com-
    pany, 1841
Houston Baptist Hospital, 1907
Houston Belt and Magnolia Park
    Railway Company, 1889, 1899
Houston Belt and Terminal Railway
    Company, 1905
Houston and Brazos Valley Railway,
    1891, 1907
Houston *Chronicle,* 1901
Houston County, 1686, 1690, 1837
Houston Direct Navigation Company,
    1866
Houston, East and West Texas
    Railway, 1875
Houston and Great Northern Railroad
    Company, 1866
Houston, Oaklawn, and Magnolia
    Park Railway Company, 1889,
    1899
Houston *Post,* 1880, 1885
Houston *Press,* 1911
Houston Railway Company, 1892
Houston Ship Channel, 1869, 1914
Houston Tap and Brazoria Railway
    Company, 1856
Houston and Texas Central Railway
    Company, 1848, 1856, 1872, 1881,
    1893
Houston and Texas Railroad Com-
    pany, 1893
Houston, Trinity, and Tyler Railroad,
    1860

NUESTRA SEÑORA de Carmen Church in Ysleta, Texas.
*— Photo from The University of Texas
Institute of Texan Cultures.*

Houstonian, 1841
Howard, Volney Erskine, 1876
Howard Bill, 1870
Howard County, 1876, 1882
Howard Payne College, 1889, 1890
Huane Indians, 1684, 1767
Hudspeth, Claude Benton, 1717
Hudspeth County, 1750, 1858, 1882, 1917
Huicasique Indians, 1684
Hull Oil Field, 1918
Humble Oil Company, 1911
Humble Oil Field, 1905
Hume Indians, 1675
Hunt, Memucan, 1846

Hunt County, 1846, 1867, 1892
Hunter's Frontier Magazine, 1915
Hunter's Magazine, 1910
Huntsville, Texas, 1841, 1846, 1848, 1879
Hunstville Academy, 1846
Huntsville Branch Railway Company, 1873
Huntsville Male Institute, 1848
Hurricanes, 1875, 1886, 1900, 1916
Huston, Felix, 1837
Hutchinson, Anderson, 1876
Hutchinson County, 1876, 1901
Huyuguan Indians, 1718

Jasper Collegiate Institute, 1851
Jasper County, 1836, 1854
Jasper and Eastern Railroad, 1904
Jaybird Democratic Organization, 1899
Jaybird-Woodpecker War, 1888, 1889
Jedionda Indians, 1684
Jeff Davis County, 1887
Jefferson, Thomas, 1836
Jefferson, Texas, 1857, 1873
Jefferson County, 1685, 1836, 1891
Jefferson and Northwestern Railroad, 1899
Jersey Cattle, 1880
Jesús María, Francisco de, 1691
Jewish Herald-Voice, 1908
Jews in Texas, 1821, 1844, 1907, 1908
Jim Hogg County, 1913
Jim Ned Creek, 1857
Jim Wells County, 1852, 1875, 1911, 1912
John B. Denton College, 1900, 1904
John Sealy Company, 1909
John Sealy Hospital School for Nurses, 1890
John T. Allen School, 1896
John Tarleton Agricultural College, 1917
John Tarleton College, 1898, 1917
Johnson, Francis W., 1836, 1840
Johnson, Gail Borden, 1880
Johnson, Middleton Tate, 1854
Johnson County, 1854, 1896
Johnson Institute, 1852
Johnston, Albert Sidney, 1837, 1856
Jones, Anson, 1858
Jones, John Rice, 1835
Jones County, 1858, 1876, 1881
Jones and Plummer Trail, 1876
Jotar Indians, 1779
Journal and Advertiser, 1840, 1841
Joutel, Henri, 1686, 1687, 1689, 1787
Judicial Counties, 1841, 1842
Juliette Fowler Homes for Orphans and Aged, 1905
Jumano Indians, 1583, 1683, 1771
Junction, Texas, 1852
"Juneteenth," 1865
Junior Colleges, 1886, 1894, 1897, 1898, 1899, 1907, 1909, 1911, 1915, 1916, 1920

K

Kabaye Indians, 1687
Kadodacho Indians, 1542
Kannehouan Indians, 1687
Kanohatino Indians, 1687
Kansas City, Mexico, and Orient Railway Company of Texas, 1900
Kansas and Gulf Short Line Railroad Company, 1880, 1891
Karankawa Indians, 1824, 1852
Karnes, Henry W., 1854
Karnes County, 1830, 1852, 1854
Kaufman, David Spangler, 1848
Kaufman, Texas, 1854
Kaufman County, 1848
Kaufman Masonic Institute, 1854
Keatchie, Louisiana, 1875
Keatchie College, 1875, 1877
Keene, Texas, 1894, 1916
Keene Industrial Academy, 1894
Kelly, Michael J., 1868
Kelly Air Force Base, 1917
Kelly Plow Company, 1843
Kelly's Stage Stand, 1852
Kelsey, Texas, 1901
Kendall, George Wilkins, 1862
Kendall County, 1862
Kenedy, Mifflin, 1867
Kenney's Fort, 1839
Kent, Andrew, 1876
Kent Colony, 1850
Kent County, 1876, 1892
Kentucky Cattle Company, 1884
Kentucky Mustangs, 1835
Kentucky Volunteers, 1835
Kentuckytown, Texas, 1865
Ker, Henry, 1816
Keremen Indians, 1687
Kerr, James, 1856
Kerr County, 1855, 1856, 1859, 1862, 1880
Kerrville, Texas, 1887, 1908, 1920
Kichai Indians, 1719, 1772
Kickapoo Indians, 1835, 1838, 1839, 1865

Kicking Bird, 1865
Kidd-Key College, 1919
Kildare and Linden Railway, 1891
Kimble, George C., 1858
Kimbell County, 1858, 1876
King, William P., 1876
King County, 1876, 1891, 1900
King Ranch, 1852
Kingston, Texas, 1880, 1887
King's Highway, 1691
Kingsville, Texas, 1911, 1912
Kinney, Henry L., 1850
Kinney County, 1675, 1850, 1852
Kiowa Indians, 1834
Kironona Indians, 1687
Kitachai Indians, 1772
Kleberg, Robert Justus, 1913
Kleberg County, 1913
Knight, H.M., 1890
Knights of the Golden Circle, 1854
Knights of Labor, 1886
Knights of Pythias, 1872
Knights of the White Camelia, 1867
Know-Nothing Party, 1854
Knox, Henry, 1858
Knox County, 1858, 1876, 1886
Knutson, Ole, 1853
Koasati Indians, 1854
Kokernot Ranch, 1837
Ku Klux Klan, 1866, 1870
Kyle Baptist Seminary, 1889
Kyle Seminary, 1884, 1889

L

LIT Ranch, 1877
LS Ranch, 1884
LX Ranch, 1877
La Baca County, 1842
La Bahía Mission, 1721, 1722
La Bahía Presidio, 1836
Labor Newspapers, 1888, 1919
Labor Statistics, 1909
Labor Unions, 1860, 1865, 1866, 1870, 1879, 1895
Lacane Indians, 1542
Lacopsile Indians, 1781
Lacy's Fort, 1835
Ladies Battalion, 1836

Ladonia, Texas, 1860
Ladonia Male and Female Institute, 1860
Lafayette, Marquis de, 1837
Lagarto, Texas, 1880
Lagarto College, 1880
La Grange, Texas, 1828, 1840, 1844, 1845, 1847, 1849, 1853, 1855, 1856, 1860, 1879, 1885
La Grange Collegiate Institute, 1849, 1853, 1855
La Grange Female Institute, 1845
La Grange *Intelligencer*, 1844
La Grange Male and Female Seminary and Boarding School, 1853
La Grange *Paper*, 1855
La Grange Preparatory School for Females, 1853, 1855
La Grange Select School, 1856
La Harpe, Bernard de, 1719
La Junta de los Rios, 1583
Lake Abilene, 1918
Lake Austin, 1890
Lake Balmorhea, 1917
Lake Creek Railway Company, 1894
Lake McDonald, 1890
Lake Mineral Wells, 1920
Lake Randall, 1909
Lake Wichita, 1901
Lake Worth, 1916
Lakes, 1890, 1900, 1901, 1909, 1910, 1911, 1912, 1913, 1916, 1917, 1918, 1920
Lamar, Mirabeau Buonaparte, 1798, 1838-1841
Lamar County, 1840, 1841
Lamar Female Seminary, 1866, 1871
Lamb, George A., 1876
Lamb County, 1876, 1889, 1901, 1908
Lampasas, Texas, 1885
Lampasas County, 1856, 1873, 1877
Lampasas River, 1856
La Navidad en las Cruces, 1683
Lancaster, Texas, 1899
Lancaster Tap Railroad, 1889
Land Board, 1883
Land Companies, 1830, 1835, 1838, 1876, 1882, 1883, 1884, 1912
Land Fraud Board, 1883

Land Grants, 1825, 1829, 1842, 1844
Land Laws, 1839, 1845, 1905
Land Sales, 1895
Landa Park, 1898
La Porte, Houston, and Northern Railroad Company, 1892, 1895
La Prensa, 1913
Laredo, Texas, 1684, 1696, 1840, 1849, 1861, 1880
Laredo Seminary, 1880, 1891
Laredo *Times,* 1881
La Réunion, 1854, 1855
La Salle, Réne Robert Cavelier, Sieur de, 1682, 1685, 1687, 1690, 1858
La Salle County, 1852, 1858, 1880, 1898
La Salle Expedition, 1687
Latimer, Albert Hamilton, 1868
Latimer County, 1868
Laura, 1837
Laureles Ranch, 1867
Lavaca County, 1846, 1861
Lavaca River, 1687, 1846
Law of April 6, 1830, 1830
League of Texas Municipalities, 1913
Leaton, Ben, 1846
Ledger, 1869, 1872
Lee, Robert E., 1856, 1860, 1874
Lee, W.M.D., 1884
Lee County, 1874
Lee-Peacock Feud, 1867
Leon, Alonso de, 1690, 1696
León Martín de, 1846
León County, 1840, 1846
Leon Springs First Officers Training Camp, 1917
Levee Improvement Districts, 1909
Liberty, 1836
Liberty, Texas, 1818
Liberty County, 1836, 1840, 1841, 1918
Liberty Hill, Texas, 1886
Liberty Normal and Business College, 1886
Liberty Volunteers, 1835
Libraries, 1839, 1874, 1883, 1900, 1904, 1905, 1909, 1914
Lighthouses, 1852, 1872
Lily-White Movement, 1884, 1896

Limestone, 1846
Limestone County, 1834, 1846
Lincoln, George, 1849
Linn, W., 1876
Linnville, Texas, 1840
Lipan Indians, 1732, 1771
Lipan-Apache Indians, 1855
Lipantitlán Expedition, 1835
Lipscomb, Abner S., 1876
Lipscomb County, 1876, 1887
Literary Intelligencer, 1844
Literary Magazines, 1898
Little Penn, 1838
Little River, 1687
Little Theatres, 1909, 1919, 1920
Little Wichita River, 1859
Littlefield, George W., 1877, 1901, 1912, 1914
Littlefield Lands Company, 1912
Littlefield Southern History Fund, 1914
Live Oak County, 1850, 1856, 1920
Live Oak Female Seminary, 1853
Live Oak Trees, 1856
Lively, 1821
Livestock Sanitary Commission, 1893
Livingston and Southeastern Railway Company, 1903
Llano, Texas, 1847, 1897
Llano County, 1856, 1873
Llano Cattle Company, 1880
Llanos-Cárdenas Expedition, 1690
Llano Estacado Institute, 1889
Llano Estacado Railroad, 1909
Lockhart, Texas, 1840, 1850
Lockhart Academy, 1850
Lockney, Texas, 1894
Lockney Christian College, 1894
Locomotives, 1852
Log of a Cowboy, 1903
London, 1885
Lone Star Salt Company, 1891
Long Expedition, 1819
Longshoremen, 1866, 1879
Longshoremen Unions, 1866, 1870
Longview, Texas, 1894
Longview and Sabine Valley Railway, 1878
Los Adaes, 1721

Los Surdos Indians, 1683
"Lost Nigger" Expedition, 1877
Louis XIV, 1682
Louisiana, 1719, 1790, 1806, 1812
Louisiana Purchase, 1806
Louisiana Western Extension Railroad, 1879
Louisville, Georgia, 1798
Love, Thomas B., 1905
Love Field, 1914
Loving, Oliver, 1887
Loving County, 1887, 1893
Lowrey-Phillips School, 1910
Loyal League, 1861
Loyal Union League, 1869
Lubbock, F.R., 1861
Lubbock, Thomas S., 1876
Lubbock County, 1876, 1885, 1891
Lubricating Oil Company, 1888
Lucas Gusher, 1901
Lufkin, Hemphill, and Gulf Railway, 1912
Lumber in Texas, 1856
Luther Rice Baptist Female College, 1856
Lutherans in Texas, 1857, 1896, 1906
Lynn, W., 1876
Lynn County, 1876, 1903

Mc

MacArthur, Arthur, 1917
McCulloch, Ben, 1856, 1896
McCulloch County, 1856, 1862, 1876
McFaddin, W.P., Jr., 1891
McIlhany, Marshall, 1898
McKavett, Henry, 1852
McKenzie College, 1841, 1848
McKinney, Collin, 1864
McKinney, Texas, 1880
McKinney, Williams and Company, 1834, 1838
McKnight State Sanatorium, 1912, 1913
McLennan, Neil, 1850
McLennan County, 1850
McMahan's Chapel, 1833
McMullen College, 1881

McMullen County, 1858, 1862, 1877, 1881
McMullen-McGloin Colony, 1828
McRae, Jim, 1869
McVeigh School, 1867

M

Macaroni Road, 1880
Macocoma Indians, 1693
Madison, James, 1853
Madison County, 1821, 1842, 1853
Magazines, 1866, 1872, 1876, 1881, 1891, 1894-1897, 1903, 1909, 1910, 1912, 1914-1918, 1920
Mahuame Indians, 1699
Mail Routes, 1857, 1858
Maliacone Indians, 1528
Mallet, Paul, 1740
Mallet, Pierre, 1740
Mallet Expedition, 1740
Malone, J.R., 1875
Mamuya Indians, 1693
Mana Indians, 1683
Manam Indians, 1690
Manico Indians, 1690
Mano Indians, 1683
Manos Coloradas Indians, 1674
Manos de Perro Indians, 1756, 1760
Manos Prietas Indians, 1718
Manos Sordos Indians, 1693
Mansion House, 1836, 1844
Manso Indians, 1659
Mantua, Texas, 1856
Mantua Seminary, 1856
Mapoch Indians, 1693
Marble Falls, Texas, 1890
Marble Falls Alliance University, 1890
Marcy, Randolph B., 1854
Marcy, William L., 1845
Marfa and Mariposa Mining Company, 1898
Margil de Jesús, Antonio, 1720
Margaret Houston Female College, 1856
Mariame Indians, 1707
Marianne Wharton College 1858, 1860
Marion, Francis, 1860
Marion County, 1860, 1898

149

HEADQUARTERS AND main station of the Texas-Mexican Railroad in Laredo as it appeared about 1925. The railroad was founded in 1881.

— *Photo from St. Mary's University.*
Copy from The University of Texas Institute of Texan Cultures.

Marshall, Texas, 1842-1845, 1849, 1850, 1854, 1856, 1862, 1863, 1865, 1873, 1881, 1882

Marshall Conferences, 1862, 1863, 1865

Marshall and East Texas Railway Company, 1908

Marshall and Northwestern Railroad, 1882, 1885

Marshall *Review*, 1843

Marshall, Timpson, and Sabine Pass Railroad Company, 1896

Marshall University, 1842, 1850

Martín Hernán, 1650

Martin, Wylie, 1876

Martin County, 1876, 1884, 1894

Martos y Navarrete, Angel de, 1756

Marvin College, 1873

Mary Allen Junior College, 1886

Mary Allen Seminary, 1886

Mary Hardin-Baylor College, 1845, 1865, 1886

Mary Nash College, 1877

Mashed O Ranch, 1889, 1891

Mason, George T., 1851

Mason, Richard Barnes, 1851

Mason, Texas, 1867

Mason County, 1858, 1862, 1875

Mason County War, 1875

Masonic Collegiate Institute, 1846

Masonic Female Institute, 1850

Masonic Institute of San Augustine, 1851

Masonic Lodges, 1850, 1856, 1871

Massanet, Damian, 1670, 1689, 1690, 1691

Matador Land and Cattle Company, Limited, 1882

Matador Ranch, 1883, 1878

Matagorda, Texas, 1837, 1839, 1843, 1846, 1849

Matagorda Bay, 1685, 1687, 1689, 1722, 1861

Matagorda *Bulletin*, 1837

Matagorda County, 1836, 1909

Matagorda Island, 1528, 1863

Matagorda Peninsula, 1864

Matamoros Expedition, 1836, 1837

Maverick, Samuel A., 1845, 1856

Maverick County, 1691, 1856, 1871

"Mavericking," 1845, 1866

Mayeye Indians, 1687, 1748

Mayo, Edward H., 1911

Meachem Field, 1914

Meat Packing, 1900, 1901, 1910

Medical Association of Texas, 1869

Medical Branch of the University of Texas, 1881

Medicine, 1837, 1853, 1869

Medina County, 1690, 1848, 1849, 1912, 1913

Medina Lake, 1912, 1913

Medina River, 1690, 1848, 1854

Medina River, Battle of the, 1813

Mellon, H.B., 1870

Melrose, Texas, 1866

Melvin, Texas, 1915

Memphis, El Paso, and Pacific Railroad, 1853

Menard, Michel B., 1858

Menard, Texas, 1757

Menard County, 1841, 1852, 1858, 1871

Mendoza, Juan Domínguez de, 1684

Mendoza, Viceroy, 1540

Menenquen Indians, 1740

Menger Hotel, 1859

Mennonite Church, 1905

Mental Institutions, 1883, 1885, 1889, 1892, 1917, 1919

Mepayaya Indians, 1691

Meracouman Indians, 1687

Mercer, Charles Fenton, 1844

Mercer Colony, 1844

Merchants War, 1850

Mercury Production, 1886, 1898

Mercy Academy, 1894

Meridian Junior College, 1907, 1909, 1920

Meridian Training School, 1907, 1909, 1920

Merrill, Hamilton W., 1850

Mescal Indians, 1689, 1716

Mesquite, Texas, 1882

Mesquite Indians, 1693, 1720

Mesquiter, 1882

Methodist Church, 1833, 1839, 1849, 1852, 1855, 1875, 1876, 1906,

Mobile, Alabama, 1835, 1836
Mobile Grays, 1835, 1836
Monclova, 1811, 1833
Montague, Daniel, 1857
Montague County, 1857, 1872
Monterrey, Mexico, 1842
Montezuma Affair, 1842
Montgomery, Richard, 1837
Montgomery, Texas, 1845
Montgomery County, 1837, 1879
Montgomery Institute, 1878
Montgomery *Patriot*, 1845
Moody, Texas, 1916
Moore, E.W., 1876
Moore, John Henry, 1828
Moore County, 1876, 1892
Moore's Fort, 1828
Morfi, Juan Agustín, 1730, 1781
Morgan Lines, 1835
Mormon Mill Colony, 1851
Mormons, 1845, 1854, 1901
Morning Chronicle, 1885
Morning Herald, 1841
Morning Star, 1839
Morrell, Z.N., 1837
Morris, Francis, 1880
Morris, W.W., 1875
Morris County, 1875
Morris Ranch, 1880
Morton Salt Company, 1920
Moscoso de Alvarado, Luis de, 1542, 1543
Moscoso Expedition, 1542
Moscow, Camden, and San Augustine Railroad, 1898
Mother Neff State Recreation Park, 1916
Motion Pictures, 1905
Motley County Railroad, 1919
Motley County, 1876, 1891
Mottley, Junius William, 1876
Mound Prairie Institute, 1854, 1855
Mount Calvary Seminary, 1869, 1870
Mount Enterprise Male and Female Academy, 1858
Mount Enterprise Male and Female College, 1851
Mount Zion Baptist Association, 1875
Muele Indians, 1683

Mulato Indians, 1784
Muleshoe Ranch, 1844
Municipality of Harrisburg, 1836
Municipality of Mina, 1836
Municipality of Sabine, 1837
Municipality of San Augustine, 1836
Murders, 1896
Murphy, Margaret Healey, 1893
Murrah, Pendleton, 1863
Muruam Indians, 1670, 1707, 1726
Museums, 1845, 1892, 1903, 1909
Musquito, 1840

N

Naaman Indians, 1690
Nabedache Indians, 1686
Nabeyxa Indians, 1691
Nabiri Indians, 1687
Nacachau Indians, 1716
Nacaniche Indians, 1719
Nacau Indians, 1690, 1716
Nacisi Indians, 1790
Nacogdoche Indians, 1716, 1836
Nacogdoches, Texas, 1543, 1716, 1754, 1779, 1819, 1821, 1826, 1829, 1835, 1836, 1837, 1841, 1845, 1870, 1875
Nacogdoches Archives, 1850, 1878
Nacogdoches County, 1716, 1836, 1888
Nacogdoches and Southeastern Railroad Company, 1909
Nacogdoches University, 1845, 1875, 1877
Nacono Indians, 1716
Nadamin Indians, 1687
Nakanawan Indians, 1872
Nasoni Indians, 1716, 1719
Nassau Farm, 1843
Natchitoch Indians, 1719, 1858
Natchitoches, Louisiana, 1798, 1813
National Bank of Texas, 1838
National Banks, 1865
National Banner, 1838
National Cemetery, 1867
National Guard, 1890
National Intelligencer, 1838, 1841
National Road, 1839
National Vindicator, 1843

Natural Gas, 1879
Naval Battles, 1836
Navarro, José Antonio, 1846
Navarro County, 1838, 1846, 1867, 1906
Navarro Refining Company, 1909
Navasota County, 1841, 1842
Navasota River, 1732
Nave-McCord Cattle Company, 1882
Navigation Channels, 1897, 1899
Navigation Companies, 1866
Navigation Districts, 1909
Nazarene Church, 1898, 1899, 1908, 1909, 1911
Neche Indians, 1687, 1716
Neches, Battle of the, 1839
Neches County, 1841
Neches River, 1690
Neches River Boundary Claim, 1836
Negro Longshoremen's Association, 1870
Negroes in Texas, 1785, 1860, 1865, 1868, 1900, 1905
Neighbors, R. S., 1858
Neiman-Marcus Company, 1907
Neu Braunfelser Zeitung, 1852
Neuthard School, 1858
Neutral Ground Agreement, 1806
New Braunfels, Texas, 1756, 1845, 1852, 1853, 1856, 1898
New Braunfels Academy, 1856, 1858
New Braunfels *Herald*, 1890
New Era, 1845, 1846
New Mexico, 1675, 1680, 1740, 1841, 1848, 1850, 1862, 1896, 1911
New Orleans, Louisiana, 1740, 1821, 1835, 1836, 1837, 1847, 1867, 1875
New Orleans Greys 1835
New Philippines, 1716
New Spain, 1776
New Washington Association, 1838
New York, 1830, 1872
New York, Texas, and Mexican Railway, 1880
Newspapers, 1813, 1819, 1823, 1829, 1831, 1832, 1834, 1835, 1837, 1838-1847, 1849, 1850, 1852-1855, 1857, 1858, 1860, 1865, 1867, 1868, 1869, 1872, 1873-1876, 1878-1890, 1892,

1894, 1895, 1897, 1898, 1900, 1901, 1906, 1907, 1908, 1910, 1911, 1913, 1914, 1917, 1918, 1919
Newton, John, 1846
Newton County, 1846
Ney, Elisabet, 1892
Nigco Indians, 1730
Nigger Horse, 1876
Niles, J. Warren, 1838, 1839
Nimitz Hotel, 1847
Ninetieth Division, 1917
Nolan, Philip, 1876
Nolan County, 1876, 1881
Nolan Expedition, 1877
Nonapho Indians, 1726
Norbdoe, Johannes, 1841
Norris, James M., 1862
North Galveston, Houston, and Kansas City Railroad, 1892, 1895
North Texas Baptist College, 1891
North Texas Educational Association, 1877, 1880
North Texas Female College, 1871, 1892
North Texas Female College and Kidd-Key Conservatory of Music, 1892, 1919
North Texas and Santa Fe Railway, 1916
North Texas State Normal College, 1890, 1899
North Texas State University, 1890, 1899
North Texas University School, 1905, 1909
Northeast Texas Railway, 1902
Northern Division of Liberty County, 1840, 1841
Northern Frontier, 1776
Northern Methodist Church, 1881
Northern Standard, 1842
Northwest Texas Baptist College, 1891, 1897
Northwest Texas Cattle Raisers' Association, 1877
Northwest Texas Methodist Conference, 1873
Norwegian Lutherans, 1896

Norwegians in Texas, 1841, 1845, 1853

Novrach Indians, 1684

Nueces County, 1846, 1852

Nueces River, 1683, 1689, 1690, 1691, 1693, 1727, 1768, 1780, 1842, 1846

Nueces Valley, Rio Grande, and Mexico Railway, 1905

Nuestra Señora de la Candelaria Mission, 1749, 1750

Nuestra Señora de la Candelaria del Cañon Mission, 1762

Nuestra Señora de la Concepción del Socorro, 1682

Nuestra Señora de Dolores, 1716, 1750

Nuestra Señora de los Dolores de los Ais Mission, 1716

Nuestra Señora de los Dolores de los Tejas Presidio, 1716

Nuestra Señora de Espíritu Santo de Zuñiga Mission, 1722, 1785, 1794

Nuestra Señora de Guadalupe Mission, 1756

Nuestra Señora de Guadalupe de Jesús Victoria, 1836

Nuestra Señora de Guadalupe de los Mansos, 1659

Nuestra Señora de Guadalupe de los Nacogdoches Mission, 1716

Nuestra Señora de Loreto Mission, 1836

Nuestra Señora de Loreto Presidio, 1721

Nuestra Señora de la Luz Mission, 1756

Nuestra Señora de la Luz del Orcoquisac Mission, 1756

Nuestra Señora del Pilar de Nacogdoches, 1716

Nuestra Señora de la Purísima Concepción de Acuña Mission, 1731, 1733

Nuestra Señora de la Purísima Concepción de los Hainai Mission, 1716

Nuestra Señora del Refugio Mission, 1793, 1807

Nuestra Señora del Rosario Mission, 1754

Nuestra Señora del Rosario de los Cujanes Mission, 1754

Nuestro Padre San Francisco de los Tejas Mission, 1690, 1716

Nuez Indians, 1683

Nukewater Creek, 1857

Nuns in Texas, 1847

O

O Bar O Ranch, 1901

O.P.Q. Letters, 1834

O2 Brand, 1888

02 Ranch, 1891

06 Brand, 1837

OX Ranch, 1880

Oakville, Texas, 1879

Oblate College of the Southwest, 1903

Obodeus Indians, 1816

Obori Indians, 1683

Obozi Indians, 1683, 1693

O'Bryan, S.G., 1862

Ocana Indians, 1674, 1691

Ocean, 1836

Ochiltree, William Beck, 1876

Ochiltree County, 1876, 1889

O'Conor, Hugo, 1767

Odin, John M., 1841, 1847

Odoesmade Indians, 1691

Oil, 1543, 1866, 1888, 1895, 1898, 1899, 1901, 1907, 1918

Oil Boom, 1911, 1918

Oil Companies, 1898, 1899, 1901, 1902, 1907, 1909, 1911, 1917

Oil Fields, 1904-1906, 1916-1918

Oil Pipelines, 1917

Oil Refineries, 1888, 1898

Oil Wells, 1913, 1918

Ointemarhen Indians, 1687

Oklahoma, 1858, 1861, 1874, 1886, 1889

Oklahoma City and Texas Railroad Company, 1901

Old Land Office Building, 1856

Old Mill, 1835

Old San Antonio Road, 1691

Old Stone Fort, 1779

Oldham, Williamson S., 1861, 1876
Oldham County, 1876, 1880, 1884
Olivares, Antonio de San Buenaventura, 1718
Omenaosse Indians, 1687
Onions, 1898
Orancho Indians, 1764
Orange, Texas, 1911
Orange County, 1852
Orange Groves, 1852
Orange and Northwestern Railway Company, 1901
Orchards, 1904
Orcoquisac Mission, 1756
Orcoquiza Indians, 1805
Order of San Jacinto, 1842
Order of the Sons of Hermann, 1861
Orejone Indians, 1731
Ororoso Indians, 1684
Orozco y Berra, Manuel, 1684, 1864
Orozimbo Plantation, 1836
Orphanages, 1879, 1880, 1887, 1889, 1900, 1901, 1906, 1910, 1919
Our Lady of the Lake Academy and Normal School, 1895
Our Lady of the Lake College, 1866, 1879, 1912, 1919
Our Lady of Victory College, 1885, 1911
Outside Groups in Texas Service, 1835
Owens, Wesley, 1859

P

Paac Indians, 1690, 1691
Paachiqui Indians, 1690
Pacaruja Indians, 1861
Pachal Indians, 1690
Pachalaque Indians, 1733
Pachaloco Indians, 1701
Pachaque Indians, 1675
Packsaddle Mountain Fight, 1873
Pacpul Indians, 1691
Pacuache Indians, 1690
Pagaiam Indians, 1684
Paguan Indians, 1690
Paguanan Indians, 1743
Paiabuna Indians, 1684
Paine Female Institute, 1852, 1874

Paine Male and Female Institute, 1874
Painted Comanche Camp, 1854
Pajalat Indians, 1730, 1731
Pajarito Indians, 1693
Pajaseque Indians, 1746
Pakana Indians, 1805
Pakawa Indians, 1703
Palaquesson Indians, 1687
Palestine, Texas, 1772, 1854, 1856
Palmito Ranch, Battle of, 1865
Palo Alto, Battle of, 1846
Palo Duro Canyon, 1541
Palo Duro Creek, 1877
Palo Pinto, Texas, 1858, 1860
Palo Pinto County, 1856, 1857
Palo Pinto River, 1856
Paluxy College, 1877
Pamaya Indians, 1716
Pamoque Indians, 1687, 1780
Pamorano Indians, 1684
Pampopa Indians, 1727
Pan-American Railway Company, 1890
Panasiu Indians, 1690
Panequo Indians, 1687
Panhandle, Texas, 1887
Pan-Handle Christian College, 1905, 1908
Panhandle and Gulf Railway Company, 1899
Panhandle *Herald*, 1887
Panhandle Railway Company, 1887
Panhandle and Santa Fe Railroad, 1909, 1914
Panhandle of Texas, 1876, 1887, 1911
Panola Banner, 1890
Panola County, 1839, 1841, 1846
Panola Watchman, 1885
Paouite Indians, 1690
Papanac Indians, 1690
Paper Production, 1911
Parantone Indians, 1794
Parathee Indians, 1816
Parchina Indians, 1736
Paris, Texas, 1852, 1853, 1866
Paris, Choctaw, and Little Rock Railway Company, 1888
Paris Female Institute, 1852
Paris Female Seminary, 1853

Paris and Great Northern Railroad Company, 1881
Paris, Marshall, and Sabine Pass Railroad, 1885, 1897
Paris and Mt. Pleasant Railway Company, 1909
Parker, Cynthia Ann, 1836, 1860
Parker, David, 1835
Parker, Isaac, 1855
Parker, John, 1834
Parker County, 1855, 1856, 1879, 1881, 1884
Parker Institute, 1881, 1884
Parks, State, 1898, 1914, 1916
Parmer, Martin, 1876
Parmer County, 1876, 1907
Parsons, Byron, 1891
Parsons' Brigade, 1862
Pasalve Indians, 1727
Pascagoula Indians, 1908
Paschal County, 1841
Pasnacan Indians, 1743, 1754
Pasqual Indians, 1708
Pastaloca Indians, 1690, 1691
Pastate Indians, 1748
Pasteal Indians, 1690
Pasteur Institute of Texas, 1903
Pastia Indians, 1720
Patacal Indians, 1727
Pataguo Indians, 1675, 1690
Patalca Indians, 1733
Patent Office, 1839
Patents, 1837, 1839
Patiri Indians, 1749
Patriotic Organizations, 1842, 1891, 1893, 1896, 1898, 1899
Patrons of Husbandry, 1873
Patroon College, 1893
Pattillo, George A., 1852
Patumaca Indians, 1733
Patzau Indians, 1684, 1690
Paul Quinn College, 1872, 1881
Pausane Indians, 1738, 1760
Pawnee Indians, 1795
Payaya Indians, 1690, 1718
Payuguan Indians, 1690, 1720
Peace Party Conspiracy, 1861, 1862
Peach Point Plantation, 1832, 1835

Peach River and Gulf Railway Company, 1904
Peacock Military Academy, 1894
Peanut Culture, 1906
Pease, Elisha M., 1853, 1855, 1857
Pecan Culture, 1919
Pecos County, 1859, 1868, 1871, 1875, 1898
Pecos and Northern Texas Railway Company, 1898
Pecos River, 1583, 1683, 1871
Pecos River Railroad Company, 1890
Pecos Valley Southern Railway Company, 1909
Pelone Indians, 1736
Peña Station, 1875
Peniel, Texas, 1899
Peniel College, 1917
Peniel University, 1911, 1917
Pennington, Texas, 1866
Pennington College, 1866, 1870
Pentecostal Church of the Nazarene, 1911
Peñunde Indians, 1683
The People, 1838
People's Advocate, 1841
People's Party, 1886, 1888, 1891
People's Press, 1919
Permanent Council, 1835
Permanent School Fund, 1879, 1883
Perry, James Franklin, 1832
Perry, Louis C., 1915
Pescado Indians, 1683
Petao Indians, 1687
Peters' Colony Rebellion, 1852
Peticado Indians, 1770
Petrolia Oil Field, 1904
Pharmacy, State Board of, 1907
Philadelphia, Pennsylvania, 1838
Phillips University, 1908, 1918
Philosophical Society of Texas, 1837
Pickett, Bill, 1854
Piedras Blancas Indians, 1693
Pig War, 1841, 1842
Pilgrim, Thomas J., 1829
Pilot Point, Texas, 1908
Pinanaca Indians, 1675
Piniquu Indians, 1718
Pink Bollworm Act, 1917

Pinole Indians, 1693
Pinto Indians, 1680, 1757
Piro Indians, 1680
Pistols, 1836
Pita Indians, 1727
Pitahay Indians, 1690, 1691
Pitalac Indians, 1708
The Pitchfork, 1909
Pitchfork Brand, 1881
Pitchfork Land and Cattle Company, 1883
Pitchfork Ranch, 1881, 1883
Plainview, Texas, 1889, 1907, 1910, 1912
Plantations, 1826, 1832, 1833, 1835, 1836, 1839, 1843, 1845, 1847, 1850, 1859, 1884
The Planter, 1843
Planter's Gazette, 1842
Plow Factories, 1843
Plum Creek Fight, 1840
Pocket, 1836
Point Bolivar Lighthouse, 1872
Point Isabel, Texas, 1846
Pojue Indians, 1684
Polacme Indians, 1693
Poles in Texas, 1818, 1900
Police, 1870, 1873
Polignac's Brigade, 1862
Political Organizations, 1851, 1854, 1869, 1884, 1886, 1888, 1891, 1892, 1896, 1898, 1906
Polk, James K., 1846
Polk County, 1846, 1854, 1908
Polytechnic College, 1890, 1914
Pomulum Indians, 1708
Ponolo, 1846
Populists, 1884
Port Arthur, Texas, 1897, 1909, 1919
Port Arthur College, 1909
Port Arthur Canal and Dock Company, 1897
Port Bolivar Iron Ore Railway, 1911
Port Facilities, 1854, 1860
Port of Houston, 1841
Port Isabel Lighthouse, 1852
Port Isabel and Rio Grande Valley Railway, 1909
Port of Sabine, 1838

Port of San Bernard, 1805
Porter, William Sydney, 1894
Portland, Texas, 1894
Post, Charles William, 1906, 1911
Post, Texas, 1880, 1906, 1911
Post on the Clear Fork of the Brazos, 1851
Post of El Paso, 1848, 1854
Post Hill, 1851
Postal System, 1835, 1836
Postmaster General, 1835
Postito Indians, 1785
Potawatomie Indians, 1852
Potomac, 1838
Potter, Robert, 1876
Potter and Bacon Trail, 1883
Potter and Blocker Trail, 1883
Potter County, 1876, 1881, 1887
Poultry Production, 1914
Powell Oil Field, 1906
Prairie View State Normal and Institutional College, 1889
Prairie View State Normal School, 1879, 1885, 1889
Precinct of Viesca, 1830
Preemption Law, 1845
Prehistoric People, 900
Presbyterians, 1829, 1837, 1843, 1848, 1849, 1852, 1854, 1869, 1883, 1889, 1890, 1891, 1893, 1898, 1906, 1908, 1910, 1911
Presidio, Texas, 1684, 1693, 1715, 1721, 1846
Presidio County, 1683, 1850, 1852, 1875, 1887, 1891
Presidio de los Dolores, 1716
Presidio de los Tejas, 1716
Presidios, 1716, 1718, 1751
Prieto Indians, 1794
Prisons, 1848, 1862, 1864
Professional Organizations, 1880, 1882, 1885, 1889, 1892, 1902, 1909, 1910, 1911, 1918, 1920
Professional Publications, 1880, 1897, 1911, 1912, 1920
Professional Schools, 1860, 1864, 1873, 1881, 1890, 1905, 1906, 1918
Prohibition, 1854, 1866, 1870, 1882, 1887, 1918

Prohibition Party, 1886
Protestant Episcopal Church, 1838,
     1839, 1849, 1914
Provincias Internas, 1776
Public Debt, 1836, 1879, 1883
Public Land, 1836, 1879, 1883, 1895
Pucha Indians, 1684
Pucham Indians, 1684
Pueblos, 1718, 1907
Pulacuam Indians, 1690
Pulaski, Tennessee, 1866
Pulaski, Texas, 1842
Pulcha Indians, 1684
Purebred Cattle, 1848
Purchasing Agent, 1836
Purisimo Concepción del Socorro, 1682
Putaay Indians, 1690

Q

Quakers, 1879, 1890
Quanah, Acme, and Pacific Railroad,
     1902, 1909
Quanataguo Indians, 1728
Quapaw Indians, 1828
Quara Indians, 1687
Quarai Indians, 1675
The Quarterly of the Texas State His-
     torical Association, 1897, 1912
Queen Victoria, 1848
Quem Indians, 1689
Quest, G.D., 1890
Queuene Indians, 1528
Quibaga Indians, 1691
Quicuchabe Indians, 1684
Quide Indians, 1683
Quien Sabe Brand, 1898
Quien Sabe Ranch, 1898
Quiguaya Indians, 1691
Quinet Indians, 1687, 1690
Quintana, Texas, 1834, 1838
Quioborique Indians, 1683
Quiouaha Indians, 1687
Quisaba Indians, 1684
Quitaca Indians, 1683, 1684
Quitole Indians, 1528
Quitman, John Antony, 1858
Quiutcanuaha Indians, 1691

R

Racial Conflict, 1917
Radio in Texas, 1920
Railroad Commission, 1890, 1917
Railroads, 1836, 1838, 1841, 1848,
     1850, 1852, 1853, 1856, 1858, 1860,
     1866, 1870-1882, 1884-1912,
     1914-1919
Rainmaking, 1891, 1911
Rains, Emory, 1870
Rains Country, 1870
The Rambler, 1841
Ramón, Diego, 1707
Ramón, Domingo, 1716
Ranch Creek, 1877
Ranchería Grande Indians, 1707
Ranches, 1837, 1844, 1852, 1859, 1867,
     1868, 1872, 1874, 1876, 1877, 1878,
     1880, 1881-1885, 1889, 1891, 1896,
     1898, 1900, 1901, 1906
Randal, Horace, 1876
Randall County, 1876, 1881, 1885,
     1889
Randall County News, 1910
Randolph College 1899
Ranger, Desdemona, and Breckenridge
     Oil Fields, 1917
Rangers, 1836, 1862
Rath, Charles, 1876
Rath Trail, 1876
Reagan, John H., 1903
Reagan County, 1878, 1903
Real, Justus, 1913
Real County, 1857, 1913
Rebellions, Uprisings, 1811, 1826,
     1852
Reconstruction in Texas, 1865, 1870
Red-Lander, 1838, 1841
Red River, 1542, 1687, 1719, 1759,
     1777, 1816, 1836, 1857
Red River Campaign, 1864
Red River County, 1817, 1835, 1836,
     1842, 1844, 1848, 1876
Red River Indian War, 1874
Red River Station, 1857
Red River, Texas, and Southern
     Railway Company, 1901
Red Rovers, 1835, 1836

PHOTO ELECTRIC street-cars of "The Laredo Improvement Company," the Hotel Hamilton's coach, and the Rio Grande National Bank of Laredo about 1890.

— *Photo by Cockrell, Laredo, Texas.*
Provided by Charles G. Downing, Eagle Pass, Texas.
Copy from The University of Texas Institute of Texan Cultures.

Rueg, Louis, 1821
Rump Senate, 1870
Runaway Scrape, 1836
Runnels, Hardin R., 1859
Runnels, Hiram G., 1858
Runnels County, 1858, 1880
Rusk, Thomas Jefferson, 1843, 1846
Rusk, Texas, 1848, 1851, 1859, 1869, 1871, 1874, 1919, 1920
Rusk Baptist College, 1920
Rusk County, 1843, 1851, 1853, 1854, 1858, 1880
Rusk County Academy, 1845
Rusk Educational Association, 1869, 1871
Rusk Masonic Institute, 1871, 1873
Rusk State Hospital, 1919
Rusk Transportation Company, 1874
Rutersville, Texas, 1870
Rutersville College, 1839, 1840

S

SMS Ranches, 1896
Sabeata, Juan, 1693
Sabinal Christian College, 1907
Sabine Advocate, 1842
Sabine Baptist College, 1858
Sabine County, 1833, 1837, 1841
Sabine and Galveston Bay Railroad and Lumber Company, 1856
Sabine-Neches Waterway, 1899
Sabine Pass, 1865, 1897
Sabine Pass Ship Channel, 1899
Sabine Pass, Battle of, 1863
Sabine Pass, Alexandria, and Northwestern Railway Company, 1892
Sabine River, 1812, 1819, 1863
Sabine Valley University, 1875, 1876
Sacred Heart Scholasticate, 1920
St. Anthony Seminary, 1905
St. Edward's College, 1885
St. Edward's University, 1885
Saint Ignatius Academy, 1885, 1911
St. Louis, Missouri, 1881
St. Louis, Arkansas, and Texas Railroad, 1886
St. Louis, Brownsville, and Mexico Railway Company, 1903

St. Louis de Caddodacho, 1719
St. Louis, San Francisco, and Texas Railway Company, 1900
St. Mary's Academy, 1874
St. Mary's College, 1889
St. Mary's Hall, 1860
St. Mary's University, 1852
St. Paul's College, 1852
St. Philips College, 1898
St. Philip's Normal and Industrial School, 1898
Salado, Texas, 1873
Salado, Battle of, 1842
Salado College, 1859, 1860
Salado Creek, 1813, 1842
Salado Springs, Texas, 1859
Salapaque Indians, 1790
Saligny, Alphonse de, 1841
Salt Creek Massacre, 1871
Salt Production, 1750, 1870, 1891, 1920
Salt War, 1870
Saltillo, Mexico, 1824, 1833
Sam Houston Normal Institute, 1879, 1911, 1915
Sama Indians, 1719
Samampac Indians, 1689
Sampanal Indians, 1689, 1755
Samuel Huston College, 1900
San Angelo, Texas, 1684, 1685
San Antonio, 1839
San Antonio, Texas, 1690, 1691, 1709, 1718, 1722, 1727, 1730, 1731, 1733, 1738, 1749, 1755, 1756, 1760, 1772, 1785, 1790, 1811, 1822, 1823, 1830, 1835, 1840, 1843, 1851-1854, 1856-1861, 1865-1867, 1881, 1884, 1886, 1888, 1891, 1893, 1894, 1895, 1897, 1898, 1905, 1910, 1913, 1917, 1918
San Antonio Academy, 1886
San Antonio and Aransas Pass Railway, 1884
San Antonio Arsenal, 1858
San Antonio Belt and Terminal Railway Company, 1912
San Antonio de Bexar Presidio, 1718
San Antonio *Evening News*, 1918
San Antonio *Express*, 1865

162

San Antonio Female College, 1894, 1918

San Antonio and Gulf Shore Railway, 1893

San Antonio *Herald,* 1854

San Antonio *Light,* 1881

San Antonio and Mexican Gulf Railway, 1850

San Antonio National Cemetery, 1867

San Antonio Philosophical and Theological Seminary, 1903, 1920

San Antonio River, 1690, 1730, 1731, 1813

San Antonio-San Diego Mail Route, 1857

San Antonio Southern Railway Company, 1908

San Antonio State Hospital 1889, 1892

San Antonio, Uvalde, and Gulf Railroad Company, 1909, 1912

San Antonio de Valero Mission, 1718, 1719, 1720, 1726, 1728, 1730, 1737, 1740, 1743, 1755, 1760, 1762, 1764, 1785

San Antonio *Zeitung,* 1853

San Augustine, Texas, 1825, 1836, 1838, 1840, 1841, 1843, 1844, 1846, 1847, 1900

San Augustine County, 1836, 1837

San Benito and Rio Grande Valley Railway Company, 1912

San Benito and Rio Grande Valley Interurban Railway Company, 1912

San Bernard, 1839

San Clemente Mission, 1684

San Esteban Lake, 1910

San Felipe de Austin, Texas, 1829, 1831, 1835

San Francisco de la Espada Mission, 1731, 1737

San Francisco de los Julimes Mission, 1684

San Francisco de los Neches Mission, 1716

San Francisco Solano Mission, 1700, 1718

San Francisco de los Tejas Mission, 1690, 1716

San Francisco Xavier de Horcasitas Mission, 1746, 1749

San Francisco Xavier de Najera Mission, 1722

San Francisco Xavier Presidio, 1751

San Gabriel, Texas, 1749

San Gabriel River, 1687, 1748

San Gabriels, Battle on the, 1839

San Ildefonso Mission, 1749, 1751

San Jacinto, 1839

San Jacinto, Battle of, 1836

San Jacinto, Order of, 1842

San Jacinto Battleground Commission, 1907

San Jacinto County, 1869, 1870

San Jacinto Society, 1893

San José de los Nazonis Mission, 1716, 1731

San José y San Miguel de Aguayo Mission, 1720, 1784, 1785

San Juan Bautista Mission, 1700

San Juan Capistrano Mission, 1731

San Juan Plantation, 1884

San Lorenzo de la Santa Cruz Mission, 1762

San Luis, Texas, 1840

San Luis Advocate, 1840

San Marcos, Texas, 1868, 1875, 1884, 1896, 1899, 1906

San Marcos Academy, 1906

San Miguel de Linares de los Adaes Mission, 1716

San Patricio, Texas, 1828, 1830, 1836, 1841, 1846

San Patricio, Battle of, 1836

San Patricio County, 1836, 1837

San Patricio Minutemen, 1841

San Patricio Trail, 1830, 1879

San Saba, Texas, 1860

San Saba College, 1885

San Saba County, 1856, 1862, 1874, 1893, 1895

San Saba Masonic College, 1860, 1863, 1885

San Sabá Presidio, 1847

San Saba River, 1856

Sibley's Brigade, 1861
Sico Indians, 1691
Siege of Bexar, 1835
Sijame Indians, 1709
Silver in Texas, 1680
Simmons, James B., 1892
Simmons College, 1892
Sinclair, John L., 1906
Singing Groups, 1854
Single Star, 1837
Siniple Indians, 1693
Sinoreja Indians, 1693
Siquipil Indians, 1731
Sisters of Charity of the Incarnate Word, 1866, 1881
Sisters of Divine Providence, 1866, 1879
Sisters of Holy Cross, 1874
Sisters of the Incarnate Word and Blessed Sacrament, 1852
Sisters of Mercy, 1875
Sisters of Saint Dominic, 1882
Sisters of St. Mary of Namur, 1873
Sister-Servants of the Holy Ghost and Mary Immaculate, 1893
Siupam Indians, 1709
Six-Pounder, 1840
Sixth Cavalry, 1870
Skidi Pawnee Indians, 1777
Slaughter, C.C., 1880
Slaughter, John B., 1880
Slave Insurrections, 1835, 1841, 1856
Slavery, 1829, 1854, 1865
Slovan, 1879
Smith, Ashbel, 1847
Smith, Erastus (Deaf), 1876
Smith, James, 1846
Smith, Morgan R., 1847
Smith, Thomas I., 1846
Smith County, 1842, 1846, 1864
Snively, Jacob, 1843
Snively Expeditions, 1843
Social Clubs, 1857
Socialist Colonies, 1854, 1855
Socialist Labor Party, 1898
Socialist Party, 1906
Socorro del Sur, 1680, 1682
Soda Lake Herald, 1845

Soldiers and Sailors Moratorium Law, 1919
Somerset, Ohio, 1882
Somervell, Alexander, 1842, 1875
Somervell County, 1875, 1877, 1889
Somervell Expedition, 1842
Song Festivals, 1853
Songs, 1903, 1906
Sonora, Texas, 1852
Sonora, Caverns of, 1900
Sons of Confederate Veterans, Texas Division, 1896
Sons of Hermann, Order of the, 1861
Sons of the Republic of Texas, 1893
Sophienburg Museum, 1845
Souanetto Indians, 1787
Soule University, 1855, 1856
South Carolina, 1809, 1861
South East Texas Male and Female College, 1876, 1878
South Galveston and Gulf Shore Railroad Company, 1891
South Plains and Santa Fe Railway Company, 1915
South Texas Baptist College, 1898
Southern Kansas Railway Company of Texas, 1886
Southern Mercury, 1886
Southern Methodist University, 1915
Southern Overland Mail, 1858
Southern Pacific Terminal Company, 1901
Southern Transcontinental Railroad Company, 1870
Southwest Conference, 1914, 1915
Southwest Strike, 1886
Southwest Texas Normal School, 1899, 1903, 1918
Southwest Texas State Normal College, 1918
Southwest Texas State University, 1899, 1903, 1918
Southwestern Baptist Theological Seminary, 1910
Southwestern Christian College, 1904
Southwestern Exposition and Fat Stock Show, 1896
Southwestern Historical Quarterly, The, 1912

165

Southwestern Junior College, 1894, 1916
Southwestern Lunatic Asylum, 1889, 1892
Southwestern Political Science Association, 1918
Southwestern Presbyterian Home and School for Orphans, 1910
Southwestern Railway Company, 1907
Southwestern Social Science Association, 1918, 1920
Southwestern Social Science Quarterly, 1920
Southwestern Telegraph and Telephone Company, 1881
Southwestern Union College, 1916
Southwestern University, 1873, 1875
Spade Ranch, 1891
Spain, 1805
Spanish-American War, 1898
Spanish Governor's Palace, 1749
Speer Institute, 1892
Spichehat Indians, 1687
Spindletop, 1901
Spring Creek County, 1841
Springtown, Texas, 1884
Springtown Male and Female Institute, 1884
Spur, Texas, 1909
Spur Ranch, 1906
The Spy, 1840
Square and Compass Ranch, 1882
Stafford, John, 1888
Stafford, R.E., 1888
Stafford-Townsend Feud, 1888
Stagecoaches, 1852, 1858, 1879
Stamford, Texas, 1906
Stamford College, 1906, 1907
Stamford and Northwestern Railway Company, 1909
Stanton, Texas, 1894
Star of the West, 1861
Starr, James Harper, 1848
Starr County, 1848
State Agencies, 1856, 1857, 1862, 1871, 1883, 1885, 1887, 1889, 1892, 1903, 1905, 1907, 1909, 1912, 1913, 1915, 1919, 1920
State Archives, 1878

State Board of Pharmacy, 1907
State Capitol, 1897
State Dental College, 1905, 1906, 1918
State of East Texas, 1852, 1866
State Fair of Texas, 1859, 1862, 1886
State Flower, 1901
State Gazette, 1849
State Home for Dependent and Neglected Children, 1919
State Hospitals, 1883, 1885, 1917
State Institution for the Training of Juveniles, 1911, 1913
State Juvenile Training School, 1913
State Lunatic Asylum, 1861
State Orphans' Home, 1887, 1889
State Parks, 1900, 1914, 1916
State Police, 1870, 1873
State of San Jacinto, 1850
State School of Mines and Metallurgy, 1914, 1919
State Schools, 1856, 1857, 1887, 1905, 1915
State Superintendent of Public Instruction, 1884
State Symbols, 1901, 1919
State Tax Board, 1905
State Times, 1852
State Topics, A Journal of the People, 1903, 1916
State Tree, 1919
State Tuberculosis Sanatorium, 1913
State of West Texas, 1852
Steamship Companies, 1835
Stephens, Alexander H., 1861
Stephens and Carter Academy, 1851
Stephens County, 1854, 1858, 1861, 1862, 1874, 1876
Stephenson, Henry, 1834
Stephenson, Joseph A., 1838
Stephenson's Ferry, 1838
Stephenville, Texas, 1893, 1898
Stephenville College, 1893, 1898
Stephenville North and South Texas Railway Company, 1907
Sterling, W.S., 1891
Sterling County, 1891
Stevenson, William, 1817
Stockton, Robert Field, 1859
Stockton vs. *Montgomery,* 1842

166

Stonewall County, 1876, 1888
Stonewall Institute, 1867
Stonewall Seminary, 1876
Storms, 1875, 1886, 1900
Street's Weekly, 1876, 1903
Strikes, 1872, 1880, 1883, 1886
Stuart Seminary, 1875
Student Organizations, 1865
Studer, Floyd V., 1907
Studies in English, 1911
The Stylus, 1912
Suahuache Indians, 1693
Suajo Indians, 1684
Suana Indians, 1693
Sugar Loaf Railroad Company, 1893
Sugar Production, 1829, 1899
Sul Ross State Normal College, 1917, 1920
Sul Ross State University, 1917, 1920
Sullivan, Augustus W., 1835
Sulphur Industry, 1854, 1909
Sulphur River, 1838
Sulphur Springs, Texas, 1886, 1894
Sulujame Indians, 1720
Suma Indians, 1684
Sumi Indians, 1719
Sunday School, 1829
Supply, 1856
Sutton County, 1900
Sutton-Taylor Feud, 1867, 1869
Svoboda, 1885
Swartwout, Samuel, 1838
Swedes in Texas, 1838, 1870
Sweet, George H., 1872
Sweet Home Colored School, 1917
Sweetwater, Texas, 1882
Sweetwater *Advance,* 1882
Swenson, S.M., 1838, 1896
Swift and Company, 1901
Swine Breeders' Association of Texas, 1889
Swine Raising, 1889
Swisher, John G., 1876
Swisher County, 1876, 1890
Swiss in Texas, 1821
Synodical College, 1890, 1893

T

T Anchor Ranch, 1877, 1885
T Bar Ranch, 1874
Tacame Indians, 1730, 1737
Tahiannihouq Indians, 1687
Tahocullake Indians, 1839
Taimamar Indians, 1675
Talion, Jean, 1690
Talion, Pierre, 1690
Tamcan Indians, 1708
Tampaquash Indians, 1855
Tamique Indians, 1749
Tanima Indians, 1801
Tanpachoa Indians, 1584
Tanpacuaze Indians, 1780, 1855
Taovaya Indians, 1759
Taracone Indians, 1723
Taraha Indians, 1687
Tarantula, 1861
Tarrant, Edward H., 1843, 1849
Tarrant County, 1849, 1850, 1916, 1917
Tawakoni Indians, 1796
Taxes, 1871
Taylor, Zachary, 1846
Taylor, Texas, 1839
Taylor, Bastrop, and Houston Railway Company, 1886
Taylor County, 1858, 1872, 1878, 1883
Taylor Family, 1858
Taylor's Trail, 1846
Taxpayers' Convention of 1871, 1871
Taztasagonie Indians, 1730
Tchanhié Indians, 1687
Teachers Organizations, 1871, 1877, 1879, 1880
Teal, Henry, 1837
Teaname Indians, 1708
Teanda Indians, 1684
Tecahuiste Indians, 1690
Tehuacana, Texas, 1852, 1869, 1873, 1902
Tehuacana Academy, 1852
Tehuacana Creek Council, 1843, 1844, 1845
Tejas Indians, 1781
Tejón Indians, 1886
Telamene Indians, 1689

Telegraph, 1854, 1856, 1866, 1870, 1881

Telegraph Companies, 1881, 1883

Telegraph and Texas Register, 1835

Telephones, 1878, 1879, 1881, 1883

Telephone Companies, 1881, 1883

Temple, Texas, 1839, 1904

Temple-Northwestern Railway Company, 1910

Temple Sanitarium, 1904

Tenawa Indians, 1850

Tenicapene Indians, 1800

Tennessee, 1786, 1795

Tennessee Volunteers, 1835

Tenu Indians, 1740

Tepachuache Indians, 1693

Tepelguan Indians, 1590

Tepemaca Indians, 1757

Terán de los Rios, Domingo, 1691

Terocodame Indians, 1718

Terrell, Alexander Watkins, 1905

Terrell, George W., 1843

Terrell, Texas, 1883, 1885, 1897, 1905, 1909, 1912, 1915

Terrell County, 1905

Terrell Election Law, 1905

Terrell State Hospital, 1883, 1885

Terrell University School, 1912

Terrett, John C., 1852

Terry, Benjamin Franklin, 1876

Terry County, 1876, 1904

Terry's Texas Rangers, 1861

Tet Indians, 1706, 1708

Tetzino Indians, 1740

The Texan, 1879

Texan Santa Fe Expedition, 1841, 1842

Texana, Texas, 1850

Texana Academy, 1850

Texarkana, Texas, 1719, 1901

Texarkana and Fort Smith Railway Company, 1885, 1897

Texarkana and Northern Railway Company, 1885

Texas, 1840, 1892, 1914

Texas A & M College, 1904

Texas A & M University, 1871, 1875, 1876, 1888

Texas Academy of Science, 1892

Texas Almanac, 1857

Texas American Legion, 1920

Texas, Arkansas, and Louisiana Railway, 1897

Texas Army, 1835

Texas Bankers Association, 1885

Texas Baptist Academy, 1905

Texas Baptist College, 1860

Texas Baptist Education Society, 1841

Texas Baptist Herald, 1865

Texas Baptist University, 1905

Texas Bar Association, 1882

Texas Brigade, 1862

Texas Business Men's Association, 1908

Texas Centinel, 1841

Texas Central Railroad Company, 1891, 1901

Texas Central Railway Company, 1879, 1891

Texas Chamber of Commerce, 1919

Texas Christian, 1878

Texas Christian Advocate, 1854

Texas Christian Advocate and Brenham Advertiser, 1847, 1849

Texas Christian University, 1895, 1902, 1911

Texas Chronicle, 1837

Texas Collection, 1883

Texas College, 1894, 1908, 1918

The Texas Company, 1902

Texas Congress, 1836, 1837, 1841, 1844

Texas Congress of Parents and Teachers, 1909

Texas Co-operative Poultry Producers' Association, 1914

Texas Cotton and Woolen Manufacturing Company, 1845

Texas Courier, 1823

Texas Cumberland Presbyterian, 1873

Texas Democrat, 1846

Texas Dental College, 1905

Texas Emigrant, 1839

Texas Engineering Experiment Station, 1914

Texas Farm Bureau, 1920

Texas Farm Bureau Federation, 1920

Texas Federation of Women's Clubs, 1897

Texas Female Institute, 1875

Texas Female Seminary, 1890

Texas Fine Arts Association, 1911

Texas Folklore Society, 1909, 1911

Texas Forest Association, 1914

Texas Forest Service, 1914

Texas Fuel Company, 1901, 1902

Texas Gazette, 1829

Texas Gazette and Brazoria Commercial Advertiser, 1832

Texas and Gulf Railroad, 1904

Texas Gulf Sulphur Company, 1909

Texas Haymakers Association, 1912

Texas Historical Society, 1894

Texas Holiness University, 1899, 1911

Texas Industrial Congress, 1910

Texas Industrial Institute and College, 1901

Texas Journal of Education, 1880

Texas Land Company, 1835

Texas Land and Development Company, 1912

Texas Law Review, 1883

Texas League of Professional Baseball Clubs, 1887

Texas Library Association, 1902

Texas Literary Institute, 1846

Texas, Louisiana, and Eastern Railroad Company, 1891

Texas and Louisiana Railroad, 1900

Texas Lutheran College, 1912

The Texas Magazine, 1896, 1897, 1909

Texas Medical Association, 1853

Texas Medical College, 1860, 1864

Texas Medical College and Hospital, 1873

Texas Mexican Industrial Institute, 1911, 1912

Texas-Mexican Railway Company, 1881

Texas-Midland Railroad, 1893

Texas Military College, 1915

Texas Military Institute, 1854, 1868, 1870, 1897

Texas Mission (Methodist), 1834

Texas Monument, 1850

Texas Monumental and Military Institute, 1856

Texas National Guard, 1917

Texas National Register, 1844

Texas Navy, 1835, 1836, 1838, 1839

Texas and New Orleans Railroad, 1856

Texas and New Orleans Telegraph Company, 1856

Texas New Yorker, 1872

Texas Outlook, 1917

Texas Pacific Coal Company, 1888, 1917

Texas Pacific Coal and Oil Company, 1917

Texas Pacific Railroad Company, 1871, 1872, 1881

Texas Panhandle, 1740, 1879, 1883, 1907

Texas Presbyterian, 1846, 1876

Texas Presbyterian College, 1902

Texas Presbyterian Home and School for Orphans, 1906, 1910

Texas Presbyterian University, 1896

Texas Press Association, 1880

Texas Railroad, Navigation, and Banking Company, 1836

Texas Rangers, 1835-1838, 1841, 1857, 1860, 1861, 1874

Texas Recognition of Independence, 1839

Texas and Red River Telegraph Company, 1854

Texas Republican, 1819, 1834, 1849

Texas Review, 1915

Texas, Sabine Valley, and Northwestern Railway Company, 1887

Texas and Sabine Valley Railway, 1892

Texas and St. Louis Company of Texas, 1881, 1886

Texas and St. Louis Railway, 1879, 1881

Texas School for the Blind, 1915

Texas School for the Deaf, 1856, 1857

Texas School Journal, 1883, 1914

Texas School Magazine, 1887, 1914

Texas Sentinel, 1840, 1841, 1857

Texas Short Line Railway Company, 1901

Texas Siftings, 1881
Texas Southeastern Railroad, 1900
Texas Southern Railway, 1897, 1908
Texas and Southwestern Cattle Raisers Association, 1914
Texas Spur, 1909
Texas State College for Women, 1901, 1903
Texas State Council of Defense, 1916, 1917
Texas State Highway Department, 1917
Texas State Historical Assocation, 1897
Texas State Labor Union, 1895
Texas State Library, 1839
Texas State Library and Historical Commission, 1909
Texas State Medical Association, 1869
Texas State Military Board, 1862
Texas State Paper, 1845
Texas State Railroad, 1896
Texas State Singing Society, 1854
Texas State Teachers Association, 1880, 1917
Texas Steam Mill Company, 1837
Texas Supreme Court, 1842
Texas Synodical Female College, 1891
Texas Times, 1842
Texas Transportation Company, 1866
Texas University, 1875
Texas Veterans Association, 1873
Texas Volunteer Guard, 1890
Texas Weekly Review, 1916
Texas Wesleyan Banner, 1849
Texas Wesleyan College, 1881, 1889
Texas Wesleyan College Academy, 1912
Texas Western Narrow Gauge Railroad, 1875
Texas Western Railroad, 1852, 1854
Texas vs. *White,* 1867, 1869
Texas Woman Suffrage Association, 1903
Texas Womans College, 1909, 1914
Texian and Brazos Farmer, 1842
Texian Democrat, 1844
Texian and Emigrant's Guide, 1835
Textile Production, 1830, 1845, 1850

Teya Indians, 1540
Theater in Texas, 1838, 1905, 1909, 1919, 1920
"Thespian Corps," 1838
Thirty-sixth Division, 1917
Thomas Toby, 1836
Thompson's Ferry, 1830
Thorp Spring, Texas, 1878, 1910
Thorp Spring Christian College, 1910
Throckmorton, James W., 1867
Throckmorton, William E., 1858
Throckmorton County, 1856, 1858, 1879
Thurber, Texas, 1888, 1917
Tidal Wave, 1900
Tigua Indians, 1682
Tiguex Indians, 1680
Tilden, Texas, 1881
Tilijae Indians, 1731
Tillotson College, 1877, 1881
Tilpacopal Indians, 1731
Timpson and Henderson Railway Company, 1909
Timpson Northwestern Railway, 1901, 1909
Tin Horn War, 1891
Tinapihuaya Indians, 1737
Tiniba Indians, 1691
Tiopane Indians, 1731
Tiopine Indians, 1750
Tishim Indians, 1683
Titus, Andrew J., 1846
Titus County, 1838, 1846
Tixemu Indians, 1683
Tlascopsel Indians, 1781
Tlaxcalan Indians, 1757
Toaa Indians, 1690
Toapa Indians, 1683
Toapari Indians, 1683
Tobacco Production, 1879
Tobo Indians, 1691
Toboso Indians, 1807
Toby and Brother Company, 1836
Tohaha Indians, 1683
Toho Indians, 1740
Tohookatokie Indians, 1849
Tojo Indians, 1690
Tojuma Indians, 1684
Tom Green County, 1852, 1867, 1874, 1912

Tonkawa Indians, 1719, 1855
Too Indians, 1690
Toon College, 1897, 1912
Toreme Indians, 1684
Tornadoes in Texas, 1866, 1902
"Tough 'Ombres," 1917
Tov Indians, 1755
The Town, 1844
Townsend, Nathaniel, 1837
Trail Drivers Association, 1915
Trails, 1839, 1846, 1849, 1867, 1876
Train Wreck Stunt, 1896
Trammel, Nicholas, 1813
Trammel's Trace, 1813
Transportation Companies, 1874
Travis, William Barret, 1809, 1836, 1840, 1917
Travis County, 1840
Travis Guards, 1840, 1851
Travis Rifles, 1861, 1873
Treasury Robbery, 1865
Treaties, 1836, 1840, 1847, 1848, 1865, 1884
Treaty of Commerce, 1839, 1840
Treaty of 1884, 1884
Treaty of Guadalupe Hidalgo, 1848
Treaty of Velasco, 1836
Trespalacios, José Felix, 1822
Trinity and Brazos Valley Railway Company, 1902
Trinity, Cameron, and Western Railroad, 1892
Trinity County, 1840, 1841, 1850, 1866
Trinity Lutheran College, 1906
Trinity River, 1716, 1721, 1850, 1916
Trinity River High School, 1856
Trinity and Sabine Railway, 1881
Trinity University, 1869, 1902
Trinity Valley and Northern Railway Company, 1906
Trinity Valley Southern Railroad Company, 1899
Tri-State College, 1901
Trube Family, 1850
Tucara Indians, 1728
Tucubante Indians, 1754
Tuleta, Texas, 1905
Tumpzi Indians, 1728
Tunica Indians, 1886

Tup Indians, 1750, 1755
Turkey Trot, 1912
Turner Hall Convention, 1892
Turney, W.W., 1891
Turnpikes, 1841
Turtle Bayou Resolutions, 1832
Tusolivi Indians, 1709
Twiggs, David E., 1861
"Twin Sisters," 1836
Two-Buckle Ranch, 1884
Two Circles Bar, 1883
Tyler, John, 1841
Tyler, Texas, 1853, 1854, 1860, 1863, 1864, 1865, 1869, 1875, 1883, 1892, 1894, 1898, 1905, 1908, 1918
Tyler Commercial College, 1898
Tyler County, 1841, 1846, 1917
Tyler Female College, 1883
Tyler Southeastern Railway Company, 1891
Tyler Tap Railroad, 1871
Tyler University, 1853, 1854
Typographical Union, 1865
Tyron Baptist Association, 1867

U

U Lazy S Ranch, 1880
Ugalde, Juan de, 1850
Ujuiap Indians, 1740, 1741
Union Academy, 1840
Union Membership, 1899
Union Sympathizers, 1861
Union Terminal Company, 1912
Unitarian Church, 1906
United Daughters of the Confederacy, 1896
United Friends of Temperance, 1870
United States Infantry, 1849
United States Senate, 1844
United States Supreme Court, 1867, 1869, 1896
University of Dallas, 1900, 1907, 1909
University of Eastern Texas, 1847
University Interscholastic League, 1910
University of San Antonio, 1888
University of San Augustine, 1837
University of Texas, 1881, 1883, 1909,

171

1911, 1915, 1919
University of Texas at Arlington, 1917
University of Texas at Austin, 1899,
  1900, 1903, 1909, 1913, 1918
University of Texas Dental Branch at
  Houston, 1905
University of Texas System School of
  Nursing, 1890
Unojita Indians, 1683, 1684
Upshur, Abel Packer, 1846
Upshur County, 1846, 1901
Upshur Masonic College, 1860
Upton, John Cunningham, 1887
Upton, William Felton, 1887
Upton County, 1887, 1910
Uracha Indians, 1764
Ursuline Academy, 1847, 1851
Ursuline Order, 1847
Utaca Indians, 1683
Utopian Settlements, 1848, 1851,
  1861, 1901, 1906
Uvalde County, 1849, 1850, 1856,
  1862, 1870, 1907
Uvalde and Northern Railroad, 1914

V

Valdez, Juan, 1720
Valentine, Texas, 1918
Val Verde, New Mexico, 1850
Val Verde County, 1857, 1885
Val Verde County Herald, 1889
Van Alstyne, Texas, 1889
Vanca Indians, 1691
Van Dorn, Earl, 1856
Van Zandt, Isaac, 1848
Van Zandt County, 1848
Vásquez, Rafael, 1842
Velasco, Texas, 1836, 1837
Velasco, Battle of, 1832
Velasco, Brazos, and Northern Rail-
  way Company, 1901, 1907
Velasco *Herald,* 1837
Velasco Terminal Railway Company,
  1891, 1901
Venado Indians, 1731, 1760
Vende Indians, 1794
Venice, Italy, 1914

Veterans Administration Hospitals,
  1920
Veterans of Foreign Wars, 1917
Veterans' Organizations, 1873, 1917
Vicksburg and El Paso Railroad, 1852
Victoria, Texas, 1846, 1848, 1858,
  1866, 1896
Victoria *Advocate,* 1846
Victoria County, 1836, 1837
Victoria Female Academy, 1848
Victoria Male Academy, 1858
Vidix Indians, 1691
Vigilante Groups, 1872
Villa de Bexar, 1718
Village Creek, Battle of, 1841
Vinta Indians, 1691
Vocational Education, 1896, 1901,
  1903
Volunteer Military Units, 1835, 1836,
  1841, 1861, 1862, 1863

W

Waco, Texas, 1771, 1856, 1857, 1860,
  1861, 1862, 1867, 1872, 1873, 1881,
  1887, 1894, 1896, 1897, 1902, 1911,
  1917, 1919
Waco Classical School, 1860
Waco County, 1842
Waco *Examiner,* 1867
Waco Female Academy, 1857, 1860
Waco Female College, 1860
Waco Female Seminary, 1856, 1860
Waco *Herald,* 1897
Waco Indians, 1843, 1854
Waco *Morning Times,* 1897
Waco and Northwestern Railroad
  Company, 1866, 1870
Waco Springs, 1837
Waco State Home, 1919
Waco Tap Railroad, 1866, 1870
Waco *Times-Herald,* 1897
Waco University, 1861, 1866
Waggoner Ranch, 1859
Waldeck Plantation, 1847
Walker, Joe, 1852
Walker, John George, 1862
Walker Robert, J., 1846
Walker, Samuel H., 1846

172

Walker County, 1846
Walker's Texas Division, 1862
Walker, Edwin, 1873
Waller County, 1873, 1898
Wars, 1850, 1875, 1891
Ward, Thomas William, 1887
Ward County, 1841, 1887, 1892
Warfield, Charles A., 1842
Warfield Expedition, 1842
Warren and Corsicana Pacific Railroad, 1899
Warwick, C.W., 1910
Washington, D.C., 1836, 1894
Washington-on-the-Brazos, Texas, 1836, 1837, 1839, 1840, 1841, 1842, 1843, 1844, 1850, 1900
Washington County, 1836, 1837, 1852, 1855, 1859, 1879
Washington County Railroad, 1856
Washington Masonic School, 1850
Washington State Park, 1900
Water Authorities and Districts, 1889, 1917, 1919
Water Engineers, Board of, 1913
Waters-Pierce Case, 1897, 1909
Waters-Pierce Oil Company, 1897, 1909
Waul, Thomas M., 1862
Waul's Legion, 1862
Waxahachie, Texas, 1873, 1902
Waxahachie Tap Railroad Company, 1876, 1881
Wayland, J.H., 1910
Wayland Baptist College, 1910
Weapons, 1836
Weatherford, Texas, 1860, 1883, 1889, 1890
Weatherford College, 1889, 1913
Weatherford Masonic Institute, 1884
Weatherford, Mineral Wells, and Northwestern Railway Company, 1889
Weatherred's School, Mrs., 1840
Webb, James, 1848
Webb County, 1757, 1848
Webster County, 1869
Webster Massacre, 1839
Weekly Citizen, 1843
Weekly Dispatch, 1843, 1888
Weekly News, 1898

Weekly Texian, 1841, 1842
Weekly Times, 1840
Wegefarth, C., 1873
Wegefarth County, 1873, 1876
Weir, R.L., 1839
Wells, James B., 1911
Wells College, 1894, 1896
Wends in Texas, 1854
Wesley College, 1905, 1909
Wesleyan Male and Female College, 1843, 1846
West Columbia Oil Field, 1918
West Fork of the Trinity River, 1916
West Texas Chamber of Commerce, 1918, 1919
West Texas Military Academy, 1893
West Texas Normal and Business College, 1895, 1898, 1911
West Texas State College, 1910
West Texas State Normal College, 1910
West Texas Today, 1918
Western Advocate, 1843
Western Baptist, 1892
Western Land and Livestock Company, 1884, 1885
Western Union Telegraph, 1854, 1866
Westminster College, 1895, 1897, 1902
Westminster Encampment, 1908
Westmoorland College, 1918
Westover, Ira, 1835
Wharton, 1839
Wharton, John A., 1846
Wharton, William H., 1846
Wharton, Texas, 1889
Wharton College, 1860
Wharton County, 1846
Wheat Production, 1879
Wheeler, Royal T., 1876
Wheeler County, 1874, 1875, 1876, 1879, 1883
Whig Party, 1851
Whip-handle Dispatch, 1836
White, B.J., 1835
White, David, 1836
White Man's Union Association, 1889, 1902
White Rock Dam, 1911
White Rock Lake, 1911

White Supremacy, 1889, 1898, 1902
Whiteman, 1858, 1860
Whitesboro, Texas, 1876, 1878
Whitesboro Normal School, 1878
Whitewright, Texas, 1885
Whitfield's Legion, 1861
Whitt, Texas, 1881
Whitt Methodist Church, 1884
Wichita County, 1858, 1882, 1913
Wichita Daily Times, 1907
Wichita Falls, Texas, 1874, 1907, 1917
Wichita Falls and Northwestern Railway Company, 1906
Wichita Falls and Oklahoma Railway Company, 1903
Wichita Falls Railway Company, 1894
Wichita Falls, Ranger, and Fort Worth Railroad Company, 1919
Wichita Falls and Southern Railway Company, 1907
Wichita Falls State Hospital, 1917
Wichita Falls and Wellington Railway Company, 1910
Wichita Indians, 1719, 1771
Wichita River, 1858
Wichita Valley Railroad Company, 1905
Wichita Valley Railway Company, 1890
Wigfall, Louis T., 1861
Wight, Lyman, 1845, 1851
Wilbarger, Josiah, 1858
Wilbarger, Mathias, 1858
Wilbarger County, 1858, 1881
Wiley College, 1873, 1882
Wilkinson, James, 1806
Willacy, John G., 1911
Willacy County, 1911
William Carey Crane College, 1885, 1889
William Robbins, 1836
Williamson, Robert M., 1848
Williamson County, 1838, 1839, 1840, 1848, 1886
Willis, Texas, 1879, 1885
Willis Male and Female College, 1885
Wilson, James C., 1860
Wilson, Woodrow, 1913, 1914
Wilson County, 1860

Winkler, C.M., 1887
Winkler County, 1887, 1910
Wiren, O.J., 1883
Wise, Henry A., 1856
Wise County, 1856, 1859
Wolfe City, Texas, 1906
Woll, Adrian, 1842
Women's Missionary Auxiliary, 1886
Women's Suffrage, 1903, 1918, 1919
Women's Christian Temperance Union, 1882
Women's Organizations, 1897
Wonder Cave, 1896
Wood, George T., 1850
Wood County, 1850
Woodland, Texas, 1876
World War I, 1919
Worth, William Jenkins, 1849
Worth County, 1850
WRR Radio Station, 1920
Wyalucing Plantation, 1850

X

XIT Ranch, 1885, 1888
Xanna Indians, 1691
Xarame Indians, 1699, 1718
Xeripam Indians, 1708

Y

Ybdacas Indians, 1708
Yellow House Ranch, 1901
Yellow Stone, 1835
Yemé Indians, 1708
Ylame Indians, 1684
Ymic Indians, 1708
Yoakum, Henderson, 1876
Yoakum County, 1876, 1907
Yojuane Indians, 1709, 1748
Yorica Indians, 1675
York Rite Masons, 1828
Young, Stark, 1909
Young, William C., 1856
Young County, 1851, 1856, 1858, 1859, 1862, 1871
Yoyehi Indians, 1684
Yprande Indians, 1762
Ysbupue Indians, 1708

MAP OF SPANISH TEXAS

175